# A SIMPLE ACT OF KINDNESS

## Ross Mueller

**CURRENCY PRESS**
The performing arts publisher

Red Stitch

THE
ACTORS'
THEATRE

CURRENT THEATRE SERIES

First published in 2022
by Currency Press Pty Ltd,
PO Box 2287, Strawberry Hills, NSW, 2012, Australia
enquiries@currency.com.au
www.currency.com.au

in association with Red Stitch Theatre

Typeset by Brighton Gray for Currency Press.
Cover shows Khisraw Jones-Shukoor, Lou Wall, Joe Petruzzi and Sarah
Sutherland. (Image by Robert Blackburn & Work Art Life Studios)

Currency Press acknowledges the Traditional Owners of the Country on which
we live and work. We pay our respects to all Aboriginal and Torres Strait
Islander Elders, past and present.

NATIONAL LIBRARY OF AUSTRALIA

A catalogue record for this
book is available from the
National Library of Australia

# Contents

A SIMPLE ACT OF KINDNESS

Act One                                                    1

Act Two                                                   34

*Theatre Program at the end of the playtext*

I acknowledge the Traditional Owners and Custodians of the lands on which I live and work, and pay my respect to Elders past, present and emerging.

The first drafts of this play were written while living and working on lands of the Wathaurong people and the final drafts were completed on lands of the Awabakal people.

I want to thank Red Stitch, Ella Caldwell, Peter Houghton and the fantastic cast and crew of the premiere production.

*A Simple Act of Kindness* was first produced by Red Stitch Actors' Theatre, Melbourne, on 23 November 2022, with the following cast:

| | |
|---|---|
| GREG | Khisraw Jones-Shukoor |
| TONY | Joe Petruzzi |
| JULIE | Sarah Sutherland |
| SOPHIA | Lou Wall |

Director, Peter Houghton
Set and Costume Design, Jacob Battista and Sophie Woodward
Lighting Design, Amelia Lever Davidson
Sound Design, David Franzke
Stage Manager, Natasha Marich
Assistant Stage Manager, Douglas Hassack
Assistant Lighting Design, Sam Diamond


*A Simple Act of Kindness* was developed through Red Stitch's INK writing program.

## CHARACTERS

SOPHIA, daughter

TONY, father

JULIE, mother

GREG, part-time DJ

Casting should reflect the cultural diversity of Australia.

## NOTES

The slash / indicates an interruption point. It creates an overlapping dialogue.

Do not accelerate the cadence, just talk over each other and listen to the responses. It informs the comedy of chaos.

## SETTING AND DESIGN

This play takes place between December 2019 and April 2020. We are in two-bedroom ten-year-old cookie cutter apartment, a long way from the CBD of Melbourne.

Marantz stereo equipment with a turntable and a box of records on the floor next to the wall. Apart from that? An Xbox and a TV and a karaoke microphone. Some mismatched stools, like a metal stool and a tiny plastic chair, that kind of thing, and a large white couch that does not make it through the door.

There are a series of self-portraits that accumulate across the time of the play and in the second act boxes and boxes from the Stonnington house are cluttering the apartment to overflowing.

## BACKGROUND NOTES

As I understand it, in 1975 the average house price in Melbourne was $19,800. The average wage was $7,600 per year. A house cost 2.6 times the average yearly earnings. In 2019 the average wage was approximately $72,000 and the average house price was $855,428. That's about 12 times the average yearly earnings.

Also (from what I understand), reverse mortgages are loans that enable homeowners aged 62 and older to convert part of their home's equity into cash. For some older homeowners, a reverse mortgage can be a good way to get some much-needed cash when their other sources of income aren't enough. But should you fail to be able to pay for any of those expenses, you'll be at risk of losing your home.

Reverse mortgages, also known as home equity conversion mortgages (HECM), have increased more than 1,300% between 1999 and 2008.

Oh, and Builders Warranty in Victoria? Warranty must be obtained for any work that is to be done that exceeds $16,000. This insurance must provide coverage for damages up to $300,000 and cover a period of six years for structural defects.

Now, I could be wrong about all of this ... but maybe that's why this play is a comedy.

This play text went to press before the end of rehearsals and may differ from the play as performed.

# ACT ONE

---

*SCENE ONE: 1ST DECEMBER—THE DEAL*

*Lights up on the empty apartment, then we hear.*

SOPHIA: [*off*] Great bones.

TONY: [*off*] Did you watch the game last night?

SOPHIA: [*off*] Do we need another Wayne Rooney?

TONY: [*off*] We need another Wayne Rooney.

SOPHIA: [*off*] What do you think of the bones?

      TONY *enters from one bedroom with a rice box.*

TONY: Looks like osteoporosis.

      SOPHIA *enters from the other bedroom.*

SOPHIA: This can work. We paint the walls and—what is that smell?

TONY: Goat. Ethiopian goat box, Kitten. This neighbourhood is a refugee
    camp. I'll be frank, I don't want you living out here in Kazakhstan.
    You just have to wait a little longer, save a little bit / more.

SOPHIA: No! This is good. A door, a ceiling. Walls.

TONY: Really ticking all the boxes.

SOPHIA: Two bedrooms! Separate kitchen. Car park and a cage.

TONY: When did a 'cage' become a selling point?

SOPHIA: We have been chasing the Market for two years! This is where
    it stops.

TONY: In Far Outer Western Laverton South?

SOPHIA: Uncle Michael says it's a growth corridor.

TONY: It's a lifetime way from Stonnington.

SOPHIA: [*re: measuring tape*] Get on the end of this. Go!

      TONY *takes tape and backs into first bedroom—disappears—*
      *while ...*

TONY: The building is ten years old.

SOPHIA: You and Mum started out in a studio with / cold water.

TONY: *In* Carlton! We were smoking pot for breakfast on a very good
    tram line.

TONY *reappears, backing on stage from the second bedroom, somehow he has circled the building or something? He bumps into* SOPHIA.

SOPHIA: What does the tape say?

TONY: It says this flat is fucking tiny.

> SOPHIA *lets go of the tape—it zips out and snaps on* TONY*'s fingers.*

SOPHIA: Why do you hate me so much?

TONY: Kitten! You are amazing! Important work with refugees, but …

SOPHIA: But what?

TONY: Lawyers get the properties.

SOPHIA: The people I work with would think this place was a palace.

TONY: This is a shithole place to live. Go back to school.

SOPHIA: Three years of law gave me six months of Rehab.

TONY: Finish what you / started. That little place in South Yarra …

SOPHIA: No. No! This is it. We have a deal. I am running out of time!

TONY: Okay! I didn't want to but you're forcing me to over share! Sophia, I'm sorry but your nonna is quite … healthy. And our family must carry this burden.

SOPHIA: What the fuck are you talking about?

TONY: That nursing home is killing me. So. You go back to school. Keep saving. And when Nonna is no longer …

SOPHIA: I have to get into the Market.

TONY: It's not my fault! They keep feeding her and she stays moist. She's a potted plant. Jesus. When I think about the village she came from. They all lived to a hundred and ninety, no electricity. This 'facility'! Soulless. Expensive. Promise me you will never put me in a home.

SOPHIA: Okay Dad.

TONY: I really would prefer it if you just kill me, okay?

SOPHIA: Take it easy.

TONY: I'm serious, I don't wanna die on a commode.

SOPHIA: So eat your prunes!

TONY: Just be a person for once in your life and say:

> 'Dad. Yes, I love you and I promise I will murder you.'
> I won't take 'no' for an answer.

SOPHIA: Okay! I promise I will murder you. You can trust me.

*We hear a crack, but* TONY *and* SOPHIA *do not.*

TONY: My girl. Thank you. Come on, I have to get back to work.

SOPHIA: I always do what you tell me. Second-hand clothes. Cut my own hair. Stash coins in a pickle jar, save, save, save! For what?

TONY: I never *told* you to do / anything like that.

SOPHIA: Yes you did! … We made a deal!

TONY: We *had* a deal. You make up stories.

SOPHIA: You were going to match my deposit. 'Dollar for dollar.'
I thought I could trust my own father. But clearly I was mistaken. Come on, I'll drive you back / to the city.

TONY: Wait, wait—a second.

*Pause.*

How much have you got saved?

SOPHIA: I can access one hundred and twenty-five thousand.

TONY: Jesus. What'd you do, rob a bank?

SOPHIA: I got a partner. We met at a fundraiser, we clicked. He was longlisted in the Archibald Prize. He's a really gifted painter and a D.J.
So, we made a commitment.

TONY: What kind of a commitment?

SOPHIA: He's a good guy. We want the same things in life.

TONY: Are you … ?

SOPHIA *smiles.*

You are?!
Oh my god! That's so fantastic! But are you sure … ?

SOPHIA: Hells yeah! Never been surer of anything in my life.

TONY: Kitten, you and *Rupert* 'clicked'. And now he's in London / and—

SOPHIA: Dad … Greg reminds me of you.

TONY: He does?

SOPHIA: Calm and smart and handsome.

TONY: So he's good with business and he makes you happy!

SOPHIA: He makes me very happy.

TONY: This is huge, this is great, does your mother know?

SOPHIA: I wanted to tell you first.

TONY: Yes! … We have a special bond, don't we?

SOPHIA: I thought so. Anyway … Let's get you back to work.

TONY: Wait. Being in love is a wonderful feeling. Isn't it? You just feel like anything is possible. You know, when I asked your mother to marry me, I bought her the biggest rock in the shop. Two months' salary. Down on one knee; 'Julie, you will make me the happiest man in the world, if you do me the honour of taking my hand in marriage.' She was a Big M girl. Where's the ring?

SOPHIA: No rings. We're pouring everything into our future.

TONY: Oh, that's smart.

SOPHIA: Family is serious business.

TONY: Family? … Geoff wants kids.

SOPHIA: Greg.

TONY: / Greg wants kids?

SOPHIA: And yes, yes … We want lots and lots of children. Manchester United supporters! A house full of little Wayne Rooneys! You can take them to games on the weekends, you are going to be an amazing poppa!

TONY: You're so full of life! You're a different person.

SOPHIA: I am sober. Better get you back to work.

TONY: But sweetheart … where are you and Greg going to live?

SOPHIA: Maybe we'll find a share house. Perhaps out in Reservoir.

TONY *walks deeper into the apartment towards the audience.*

TONY: This place … good bones and a cage. A growth corridor …
Let's make an offer.

SOPHIA: But Nonna is still breathing … Are you sure?

TONY: You only get one chance to start your lives together.

SOPHIA: We've got a deal?

TONY: For you … I will make this work.

*Latin music.* TONY *disappears.*

GREG: [*off*] Sophia! My saviour!

*SCENE TWO: POST-DEAL—EVENING*

GREG *in doorway. Sixpack of Stone and Wood and a UE Boom.*

SOPHIA: [*speechifying*] To getting into the Market! It's a little dark, but we can open it up!

GREG *hands* SOPHIA *beer.*

GREG: It's bad luck if you don't drink! Separate kitchen amazing!
Your room, my room. Sophia, this is perfect! Thank you sooo much!

SOPHIA: It was a steal.

GREG: The view! A view! I part-own part of a view of a … what is that?

SOPHIA: I think it's a fertiliser plant.

GREG: Love it! [*Chanting.*] I love fertiliser! We love fertiliser!

*They chant and dance 'We love fertiliser!' five or six times, then …*

SOPHIA: Greg! Wait, wait, wh-aaay-it. There is just one tiny detail …

GREG: I knew it.

SOPHIA: I don't think you do.

GREG: You want the bigger bedroom. You deserve it! It's okay.

SOPHIA: No, no. Look, it is actually kind of funny.

GREG: I'm listening.

SOPHIA: My father may think … you and I are … This is a funny story …

GREG: What does your father think Sophia?

SOPHIA: My father may think we are engaged.

GREG: Engaged in what?

SOPHIA: —To each other.

GREG: Don't get it.

SOPHIA: To be married.

GREG: To be a what?

SOPHIA: Man and wife.

GREG: Me and you?

SOPHIA: Yes.

GREG: And why the mother fuck would your father *think* a thing like *that*?

*The music stops..*

SOPHIA: He was up in my grill, telling me about my grandmother and it kinda spiralled.

GREG: You told me you had / a deal.

SOPHIA: I know! And he was backing out *again*—and so I just stopped him.

GREG: By telling him that we are getting married.

SOPHIA: Yes. And having lots of children.

GREG: Excuse me, what?

SOPHIA: I told him what he wants to hear, and he made an emotional decision and we got what we wanted. Okay? Congratulations. Isn't it great?

GREG: No. I think this is fucking insane.

SOPHIA: But we got it for under asking!

GREG: You lied to your father about us.

SOPHIA: It's just a story. He is matching our deposit dollar for dollar. We got in! Property owners.

*Beat.*

I don't want this to be a downer.

GREG: I'm sorry, but nowhere in my life plan, do I agree to marry a woman.

SOPHIA: Oh. So, this is all about you now, is it?

GREG: We are business partners, Sophia! Nobody said anything about babies!

SOPHIA: Big picture, Greg! Fuck! We just have to pretend to be a happy hetero-couple and then when we want to liquidate, we sell and spilt the profits. Trust me. People can stay engaged for years.

GREG: Can't do it. Won't do it. Forget it.

SOPHIA: Too late. Contracts are signed.

GREG: —*I* haven't signed anything!

SOPHIA: Can I just say; I am really surprised by this response.

You told me you were desperate to get into the Market and you would do whatever it takes / and …

GREG: You lied to / me!

SOPHIA: Do you want to be a forever renter? Because that is what will happen to people like you. You end up with nothing at all.

GREG: I transferred a lot of money into your account. The bank was freaking out! They think you are scamming me!

SOPHIA: I got you two bedrooms and a cage! The people I work for would kill for this! But you want out. Fine. Easy. That's it. Goodbye. Your name isn't on the papers. You don't exist.

*Pause.*

What do you want the rest of your life to look like?

*GREG walks around the apartment and examines the view. Then ... .*

GREG: I wanna make money in my sleep.

*Music: 'Saturday Night's Alright for Fighting' Elton John. SOPHIA drinks. Music continues. SOPHIA starts to dance, GREG disappears.*

## SCENE THREE—26TH JANUARY—TAKING POSSESSION

*Elton John, from an LP on the turntable of a Marantz stereo. It is basically a furniture-free apartment, but SOPHIA starts setting up the TV and Xbox. GREG carries big old speakers, albums, bubble wrapped artworks, some pots and pans, then exits to organise the sofa.*

*JULIE arrives, dressed for an Elton John concert and holding a large bunch of flowers. She kicks off her shoes and SOPHIA runs to greet her mother. They hug and start to dance together in the apartment. Singing at the top of their voices, together. The sofa topples into the doorway. GREG is struggling to make it fit.*

SOPHIA: The records are amazing, Mum!

*Needle scratch, the record stops.*

JULIE: Well, your father doesn't play them anymore.

GREG: [*off*] Little help!

JULIE: Sophia, these flowers need a vase, then I need to pick your brain.

SOPHIA: The vase could be anywhere.

GREG: [*off*] Hello?

JULIE: [*to SOPHIA*] Improvise. What do you use to preserve your stone fruit?

GREG: [*off*] The door is not wide enough!

JULIE: What was that?

SOPHIA: That's Greg.

JULIE: That's Geoff?

GREG: [*off*] Greg!

SOPHIA: Greg! / My fiancé!

JULIE: Oh! Greg! Yes! Gimme the story darling, how did he propose?

SOPHIA: Great question.

JULIE: One knee? Or did he hide the ring in your meal?

SOPHIA: No—it was, well it was very elaborate and romantic.

JULIE: Did he use a sky writer? Hire a plane? Gimme details!

GREG: [*off*] I have to leave it here.

SOPHIA: Take the legs off.

GREG: [*off*] I commissioned this couch. It's carved out of one piece of timber.

JULIE: Well, it's hard rubbish now. Just chuck it, forget it. Ohh look, fertiliser!

> GREG *laughs too long.* JULIE *hates this and makes a face at* SOPHIA. GREG *crawls over the sofa and steps into their space.*

GREG: [*to* JULIE] You must be Julie.

JULIE: [*to* GREG] Geoff! Congratulations.

SOPHIA: / Greg.

JULIE: Greg. Yes.

GREG: Thank you. So great! Two bedrooms—

JULIE: And *two* queen-sized beds. Is that for all the sex?

SOPHIA: Jesus, Mum.

JULIE: Loosen up. When your father and I were first married, you needed a crowbar to get him off me.

GREG: The extra bed is for guests.

> GREG *picks up some of the records.*

JULIE: Guests, Geoff? / Greg.

SOPHIA: Greg … Like when you and Dad want to come and stay the night.

GREG: —And have lots of sex, like Bryan Ferry.

JULIE: I'm not coming all the way to Kazakhstan for a root. No. This flat is *your* decision. For your impending marriage. Good luck with that.

GREG: [*re: the records*] Lotta records. Ohhh K-Tel! Pray tell?

JULIE: My husband bought this stereo for *a thousand dollars*. Paid by cheque. We had friends and we would sit around all night and listen to recordings of popular music. We would lounge in the lounge room and listen to the first side, the 'A-side' of the record and talk about the songs and then at the end of the first side—one of us would get up—go to the turntable and turn the record over to the other side. The 'B-Side'. And then we'd smoke another J and listen to the second side of the record. Yeah … When it was late in the evening—

GREG: Is this when you put your keys in a bowl?

JULIE: In my day we were all conversationalists. We had friends who could tell stories, whereas now? Most of those cunts are dead.

> *Beat.* JULIE *laughs loud.*

You'll get used it Geoff. I will grow on you.

SOPHIA: Champagne! Who wants champagne?! Greg? Let's get everybody a drink of alcohol to celebrate our property! Happy, happy, happy!

> GREG *begins to organise champagne.*

JULIE: So! *Greg*, tell me all about your proposal.

GREG: My proposal?

JULIE: To Sophia. Sounds like a great story.

GREG: Well, it was a pretty—routine.

SOPHIA: No, it wasn't.

GREG: Pardon me?

SOPHIA: It wasn't routine.

JULIE: Sophia just told me it was elaborate and romantic.

GREG: Yes. Elaborate and romantic in a routine, kind of way. Yes.

JULIE: Elaborate, routine, romantic? Which one was it?

SOPHIA: Mum, this is your first time in our apartment. Do you *love* it?

JULIE: What's going on?

GREG: Simple question, do you like the apartment or not?

JULIE: I think it's very dark in here.

SOPHIA: But if we put in a skylight.

JULIE: There are three flats above you.

GREG: But if we open these / windows …

JULIE: I was *not* consulted in the purchase of this flat. Your father made another unilateral, emotional decision.

SOPHIA: It's not a flat, it is an apartment.

> SOPHIA *receives a text message.*

JULIE: What's the difference?

SOPHIA: About four hundred K.

> GREG *pops the cork and pours.*

GREG: Champagne!

JULIE: You should be on apple juice, Sophia.

SOPHIA: Quick toast and then I've gotta work. / I just want to say—

JULIE: Oh! That's just great!

SOPHIA: Sorry Mum, I am toasting and then I have got work to do—

JULIE: No work! Australia Day is a public holiday.

SOPHIA: Not for people seeking asylum. Four families in a week.

JULIE: You're not even listening.

GREG: [*running distraction*] Hey Julie. What do you think of me?

> GREG *points to a large self-portrait of himself leaning on the wall.*

JULIE: Who did that to you?

GREG: Self-portrait.

JULIE: You painted yourself? Sounds like cheating.

SOPHIA: All the greats do it. Van Gough, Kahlo. Warhol. Whitely.

JULIE: And Geoff? / Greg.

GREG: Greg.

JULIE: Did your selfie win the Archie, Greg?

GREG: I'd love to paint you. I know you want it.

> SOPHIA *looks up to see* GREG *and* JULIE. *They look weird.*

JULIE: Have you got that vase yet?

> SOPHIA *finds a jar full of coins. She pours the coins out on the floor. Puts the flowers in the empty jar.*

JULIE: They need water. They are dying.

SOPHIA: [*unsure*] Nobody move.

> SOPHIA *exits with the flowers and jar.* JULIE *and* GREG *are alone. The following is a fiercely whispered exchange.*

JULIE: I don't know what your game is yet, but Sophia is mine. Understand?

GREG: I can read you like a book!

JULIE: Where's the ring Picasso?

GREG: [*re: the apartment*] Behold our commitment!

JULIE: [*displaying her rings*] This is money! This is what counts.

> She starts picking up the coins on the floor, while she continues ...

When Tony and I were your age we had nothing but the breath in our lungs. We didn't start off with a handjob from our parents.

GREG: I think you mean 'hand*out*'.

JULIE: We had nothing, Greg! Absolutely nothing!

GREG: Not even a hand job.

JULIE: Nada. Nietzsche. Nothing.

GREG: 'Nietzsche' is not the German for 'no'.

JULIE: Your personal attacks are like water off a duck's dick, to me.

GREG: I am not attacking you!

JULIE: I am pinned to the wall with your political correctness.

GREG: Your face is red.

JULIE: —Only because you decided to live in a fucking furnace.

> SOPHIA *enters with champagne and the flowers in the jar.*

SOPHIA: Thanks for your help Mum, but you don't have to be here.

JULIE: Australia Day has always been a day for celebration, / so ...

GREG: Invasion Day.

JULIE: Oh fuck off.

SOPHIA: Why are you so bloody angry?

JULIE: Because I am standing for Parliament! And *you* are helping me!

SOPHIA: I'm doing what?

JULIE: Strap yourself on, baby!

GREG: Pardon me?

JULIE: 'Strap on for Stonnington!' My slogan.

SOPHIA: 'In' ... You mean 'strap in'.

JULIE: 'On' is on-trend. I've been trolling the Greens' Facebook page for months and all they talk about is Labor, lawyers and strap-ons.

SOPHIA: I can't believe you're standing for the Greens.

JULIE: I'm not. I said I was *trolling* them. I am the maverick Independent!

GREG: Can I just say; I would so love to do some campaign posters for you.

JULIE: / Oh really? That sounds intriguing.

SOPHIA: No, you would not. Forget it!

GREG: What's your agenda, Julie?

JULIE: I am saving Stonnington! We live in a suburb that used to have walls, and now those walls have to be guarded. Who's gonna do it? You weep for the loss of your smashed avocadoes, and you curse the baby boomers. You have the luxury of not knowing what I know! My existence, while grotesque and incomprehensible to you, has helped you buy your first home. You don't want the truth because deep down in places you don't talk about at parties, you want me on that wall, you need me on that wall! I am the independent maverick! And Sophia is Communications and Fundraising.

*She hands the phone to* SOPHIA.

GoFundMe account. Ready, set, go!

SOPHIA: People won't just give you money.

JULIE: I just got three hundred bucks off your floor.

SOPHIA: That's *my* money.

JULIE: And you literally just *threw* it away! Now, hook me up. Everyone you work with will GoFundMe because I am a progressive!

*Bang!* JULIE *slides her phone over to* SOPHIA.

GREG: What makes you so progressive?

JULIE: Imagine *me* in my pyjamas!

SOPHIA: No. God. / Please. Stop …

JULIE: Perched upon an orange box of dreams. Tony and I had travelled. We went to Kathmandu before it came to Smith Street. Carlton was our universe. Rising damp and Greer and Nin! Toto's, La Mama! No wi-fi, no logo! One night after a meeting of the North Lygon Street Fabian Poets Union, Barry Dickens came over for a bong and he ate all our ginger snaps! We lived within our means, and that's how we got into the Market! Cheap wine, baked beans and we fucked on the floor.

GREG: Oh.

JULIE*'s phone gets a text message.*

SOPHIA: [*re: message*] My father is coming.

I find this whole performance deeply problematic.

JULIE: Come on darling, put your talents to good use on me.

SOPHIA: Mum. I can't. I won't give you access to my professional networks.

JULIE: Because?

*A cracking noise.*

GREG: Because she quit.

JULIE: She what?

GREG: She quit her job.

JULIE: Sophia?

GREG: It's true. She quit.

JULIE: You quit?

GREG: That's it.

JULIE: You quit your job? You love your job.

SOPHIA: I quit my job! So what?!

JULIE: What happened?

GREG: Well. It's a very funny / story …

JULIE: I want to hear this from her. What happened? Tell me. Go.

SOPHIA: I … offered my resignation and they accepted.

JULIE: That's it? / That's the story?

SOPHIA: That's it! Crazy. But sadly now, I can't give you access to my networks, because I do not have a job.

JULIE: I do not believe you do not have a job.

SOPHIA: Mum. You know what it's like when you get to a bend in the river. Something inside bursts open and … I want to live.

*Beat.*

JULIE: Is it cancer? Darling, *please* don't say it's cancer. I couldn't bear to watch you suffer while you have an enormous mortgage to service.

SOPHIA: It's my life.

JULIE: You live for your job, you are defined by what you do for a living!

GREG: That is an ancient paradigm Julie. Sophia has progressed.

JULIE: I will not be lectured about sexism and misogyny by this man! [*To* SOPHIA] I know you are lying to me.

GREG: My fiancée is not a liar!

SOPHIA: Greg.

GREG: I've got your back babe!

SOPHIA: Honey! I appreciate it. Now. Can you give us a minute? … Please?

GREG: Okay. But I am your fiancé, and I am here for you. Even when I'm in the kitchen. I am here. I mean, I'll be in there. But while I'm in there, I am here. For you. I got you, babe. I gotchew. Nobody move.

GREG *exits to the kitchen. Awkward silence.*

JULIE: This place is not big enough for a nuclear family.
It is a thimble, a shoebox. A coffin.

SOPHIA: It is not a fucking / coffin!

JULIE: Four adults in here is a crime scene.

SOPHIA: Better than a refugee camp.

JULIE: For fuck's sake! Sophia! No ring. No details. Please!
We gave you two a *lot* of money for this place and … all right.
Convince me. How did Greg propose? Did he get down on one knee?

SOPHIA: Yes. He got down / on one knee.

JULIE: Did he really? He got down on one knee.

SOPHIA: *Do not* be mean to Greg!

JULIE: Rupert is very successful.

SOPHIA: Rupert tore the heart out of my chest. Greg sewed me back together.

JULIE: That is a revolting image.

SOPHIA: He saved my life.

JULIE: You don't need a man to do that.

SOPHIA: You were going to let me choose the colour of my bedroom / wall.

JULIE: Oh, Jesus! Not this again.

SOPHIA: You told me you were leaving Dad, we were / leaving together and we were going to get a red-brick semi-detached in Brunswick.

JULIE: I never said this … No … None of this is true.

SOPHIA: We did an inspection.

JULIE: You make things up. You / make up these … stories.

SOPHIA: You said I could have the bedroom with the fireplace, and I could choose the colour for my walls and then you stayed. You never left!

JULIE: Rupert married a merchant banker. Looks like Amal Clooney. They own a three-bedroom apartment in Chelsea—and it has a rooftop fucking garden. *Three* bedrooms, two and a half bathrooms, now *that* is a property with girth.

SOPHIA: How do you even know that?

JULIE: We *like* Rupert. We stay in touch.

SOPHIA: Punch me in the throat, Mum! / Go on! Hard as you can! Just do it!

JULIE: I'm not going to do that again, I'm not! … Your eyes get small when you're histrionic. Rupert has failings, but he is always polite to me!

SOPHIA: Rupert is a narcissistic prick.

JULIE: Yes, but why did you let him go?

SOPHIA: I didn't let him go.

JULIE: Well, he's not here now.

SOPHIA: Rupert. Dumped. Me. While I was in Rehab.

JULIE: Congratulations on your emancipation.

SOPHIA: [*deflecting*] Shit Mum! *What* have you done with your hair?

JULIE: My hair?

SOPHIA: Yeah. You. Look. Hot.

JULIE: Well. It's just a rinse.

SOPHIA: Mind blown. Totally! And your arms. You're lithe. So *young*.

JULIE: / So young?

SOPHIA: Like a twelve-year-old boy.

JULIE: Well … I do Pilates and walking group.

SOPHIA: It shows. Give us a twirl.

JULIE: A twirl? / No. no.

SOPHIA: Little spin. Come on … I want to see you.

*Beat and then* JULIE *gives 'a twirl'.*

Man. You've got to get back into the business.

JULIE: / No, no.

SOPHIA: Make the calls. You are a MILF.

JULIE: Sweetheart.

SOPHIA: Mumma. Listen. I'm your girl. I am in.

*Pause*—JULIE *considers this with a genuine connection.*

JULIE: Get a pre-nup. If I had my time …

TONY *appears atop the couch, he is dressed in a crumpled Flight Centre business suit. He has been drinking.*

You have to make a wise investment, in order to profit in the end. For me, your father was the worst house in the best street.

TONY *tumbles in,* SOPHIA *runs to help him.*

SOPHIA: Fucking hell. Dad.
TONY: There's a couch in your doorway.
GREG: [*entering with a platter*] Tony!
TONY: I am bleeding! I am bleeding!

TONY *is emotional.*

SOPHIA: We've got blood people! His head is bleeding!
JULIE: Icepack! / He's not a clotter!
TONY: / I am not a clotter.
SOPHIA: He doesn't clot! First Aid kit in the bathroom.

SOPHIA *and* JULIE *exit to the bathroom for medical supplies.*

TONY: Are they gone?
GREG: Yes.
TONY: Are you okay?
GREG: Are *you* okay?
TONY: Listen to me, carefully. Are you listening?
GREG: Yes, I'm listening.
TONY: Are you listening carefully, Greg?
GREG: That's right. What's wrong?
TONY: I am completely and utterly fucked.
GREG: Ouh. Really?
TONY: So fucked I cannot see straight.
GREG: Wow. That's pretty fucked.
TONY: Yes! Deeply fucked, am I .
GREG: But … you're still going to match Sophia dollar for dollar, right?

TONY *grabs* GREG *by the shirt.*

TONY: Listen! To me!
GREG: I am listening!
TONY: Listen!
GREG: To you!

TONY: Today … I lost … my … job.

GREG: Oh fuck.

TONY: Oh yes.

GREG: Have you told Julie?

TONY: No. I have not. And I will not—and *you* cannot tell the women.

GREG: Why are you telling me?

TONY: We are men. We live in pain.

GREG: Do we have to?

TONY: Listen! / To me.

GREG: Oh for fuck's sake.

TONY: Greg! When I was your age, I was a coke dealer.

GREG: I knew it.

TONY: Sales Rep for Coca-Cola.

GREG: Okay.

TONY: Outta the blue one day I lost my job to the Fanta guy. I didn't breathe a word to Julie. She would've had a mental breakdown. I was staring into the browneye of bankruptcy. Wife and child and do you know what I did? I took them out to Gippsland. Tried to build a mud brick house and holy fuck. It almost broke me. Those bricks are tricky.

    I cannot go through the humiliation. Please. Do not breathe a word.

GREG: About what?

TONY: Me, losing my job!

GREG: I know, I was just—demonstrating that I can be trusted.

TONY: But can I trust you?!

GREG: Yes. We have a deal.

    TONY *wipes blood onto his hand and offers to shake with* GREG.

TONY: In blood.

    GREG *is weirded out, he spits in his own hand, and they shake.*

What do you know about Bitcoin?

SOPHIA: [*entering*] Icepack—

GREG: [*with huge relief*] Icepack for Dad!

TONY: Kitten … Are you happy?

SOPHIA: Mum's been here for an hour.

TONY: I'm so sorry. Darling. I love you so much. But Far Western Outer Southern Laverton is a long way from the CBD. Even for a travel agent.

GREG *laughs long,* JULIE *enters organising a bandage for* TONY.

GREG: Dad's a travel agent—

TONY *spots the stereo.*

TONY: My stereo precedes me.

JULIE: Why are you bleeding so much?

TONY: China virus! It's all a hoax. Head office are hysterical and *that's* what I told them when they were announcing the redundancies. Then farewell drinks. So you can imagine.

TONY *tries to kiss* JULIE, *who holds him back.*

JULIE: Redundancies … ?

TONY *gets a text message from Michael.*

GREG: [*distracting*] Tony, get out here and help me with the couch.

TONY: Bring me a bottle of whiskey!

JULIE: What's going on?

TONY: 'Uncle Michael' has dropped us. Oh! Michael is such a pricktease.

JULIE: Don't call my brother a pricktease. He has *major* commitment issues.

TONY: He couldn't commit to a coma. Now, I'm stuck with four hundred bucks of Elton John tickets.

GREG: Come and help me with the couch!

TONY: I gave you my stereo, my record collection and a hundred and twenty-five grand and now you want me to move your couch?

GREG: I am getting you out of the room for your own good!

JULIE: One hundred and *twenty-five*? You told me *fifty.*

TONY: Yes. Funny story about / that …

JULIE: Tell me … about the redundancies.

Beat.

TONY: Okay. So … This is a funny story sweetheart. Today? … Julie, you are going to laugh so hard … Okay. So, today … I lost my job.

GREG: Man, you just caved.

JULIE: [*to* GREG] You knew about this?

TONY: / No.

GREG: Yes.

TONY: / Yes.

GREG: No.

JULIE: What kind of package do we get?

TONY: Trust me. This is going to be like annual leave. Travel will be back in business in a few days. This virus is nothing to worry about.

JULIE: Twenty years of service and no reward for loyalty?

SOPHIA: [*making a toast*] I want to make a toast to …

GREG: Taking possession!

SOPHIA: To property! Who said it's a crime? It brings families closer together. It provides a ballast for an uncertain future. I mean, look at us. Two fiancés, living the dream. I knew it was going to be weird, but … Here we are! I did everything you told me Mum. Took all your advice and I am in. We got in! [*Calling to the entire building*] We are fucking in, my bitches!

GREG: Kah-link!!

> SOPHIA *and* GREG *laugh and drink. Cracking.* GREG *tops them up while …*

JULIE: Your father is redundant, and this is the best speech you've got?

GREG: I thought it was pretty good.

JULIE: Taking possession. On Invasion Day? Greg? …

SOPHIA: No need to get / personal.

JULIE: Oh! What if I wanna get personal? Because personally? I gave you more money than I had any idea about, my bitches. One hundred and twenty-five thousand dollars! And what have you got to say to me—for that?

> *Beat.*

I will wait all night if I have to.

> *Pause.*

Nothing to say?

SOPHIA: You are making me feel like a criminal.

JULIE: I am?

SOPHIA: I did not steal your money.

JULIE: —And yet you 'feel' like a criminal.

SOPHIA: Stop it, now!

JULIE: We built our lives around the adoration of you.

SOPHIA: Another colossal exaggeration!

JULIE: One hundred and twenty-five thousand dollars should buy me one little word! One, word!

> *Pause.*

GREG: Just say it.

SOPHIA: Congratulations.

JULIE: 'Congratulations'? …

TONY: Thank you, Kitten. /

JULIE: No! Tony! / That's not the word.

TONY: What? …

JULIE: [*to* SOPHIA] One word Sophia, is it really going to kill you?

SOPHIA: I think it might, yes. I think that's exactly what you want to happen.

JULIE: Did they teach this in Rehab? / I cannot believe you're so petty!

SOPHIA: Oh! Dredge the pits of my depression for your personal entertainment!

> TONY *spots a large crack running down the middle of the living room.*

TONY: Who did this?

> TONY *brings attention to the crack, the family gather.*

JULIE: Holy shit.

GREG: That is a fucking big—

SOPHIA: Crack.

> *A whale scream! Lights snap—*JULIE, GREG *and* TONY *disappear.*

## SCENE FOUR: 10 P.M.—MIDNIGHT—A RABBIT HOLE

*Whale moaning, scream—and building noises.*

SOPHIA *is lit by the light in the crack, the crack grows and pulsates throughout.*

SOPHIA: My parents go to the Elton John Tribute show, yes it's a tribute show, I thought it was the real thing too, but no. Apparently they prefer the fake, doesn't matter. Greg goes 'running' to deal with the stress and I am alone in this apartment for the first time. The noises are louder, the darkness is darker and the crack is getting wider by the second. I search 'concrete cracks' and this leads me to the hellscape rabbit hole of structural engineering. It is fascinating and terrifying. Architecture is all about the skin, the aesthetic enhancement, whereas a structural engineer is all about the bones of the building, this is where the rot will grow and the body will collapse, this is the most important part of the apartment block, if you get the loads wrong or the pour is not right, you are deeply, substantially fucked. Our crack is a classic two-fister. Rust and bubbles and expansion and without immediate forensic attention we will be sleeping in the rubble of debt. I text my father at the fake Elton John show: 'TONY! WE HAVE TO TALK TO IMMEDIATELY.' What have you done with Mum?!

## SCENE FIVE—THIS IS MIDNIGHT

TONY *appears next to* JULIE, *three empty bottles of champagne are on the floor. An empty pizza box. Some ice cream. No couch.*

TONY: She's in the car. Told her I left my laptop up here.

SOPHIA: You don't have a laptop.

TONY: Like she knows. Three bottles of champagne. What's up?

SOPHIA: Things are … not good.

TONY: Oh fuck. I knew it! Greg has left you, already! What a little shitstain!

SOPHIA: Dad. No. He hasn't. He's out running.

TONY: He hasn't left you?

SOPHIA: No.

TONY: Yeah. Good guy. We like Greg.

SOPHIA: Dad.

TONY: You look petrified.

SOPHIA: We have to hire a forensic engineer immediately.

TONY: You dragged me out of 'Crocodile Rock' for that?

SOPHIA: Listen. To me. Tony! Are you listening? To me! This crack is serious.

TONY: Kitten. Concrete cracks.

SOPHIA: I have researched this! We have cancer.

TONY: … Say again.

SOPHIA: We. Have cancer.

TONY: What? … All of us?

SOPHIA: Yes. The whole family has cancer. Yes.

TONY: And. You got this from Doctor Google?

SOPHIA: The floor is crumbling, there is moisture. Rust stains.
     This building is over ten years old.

TONY: Exactly!

SOPHIA: And that is a very bad thing!

TONY: How can age be bad? / Great bones! … A cage … A little paint job and … what? … What are you saying?

>    SOPHIA *reads from the phone.*

SOPHIA: 'Usually concrete cancer is prevalent in buildings that are older than ten years old. If your building is more than ten years old, you should be hyper-aware of the signs!'

TONY: 'Hyper-aware' is very emotive language.

SOPHIA: 'The most notorious signs include cracking, crumbling, rust marks, leaks and bubbling, and expansion outwards!' Tick, tick, tick, tick! And the best thing? Ten years or older? Outside the Builders Warranty.
     No. Insurance. Neitzke. You bought a lemon. Congratulations.

>    *Beat.*

TONY: People should have to disclose these things.

SOPHIA: What did it say in the structural engineer's report?

TONY: Those reports cost a lot of money Sophia.

SOPHIA: Did you get a report done or not?

TONY: Did you?

SOPHIA: You're blaming me for this!

TONY: You live here. This is / your apartment.

SOPHIA: Our investment!

TONY: But this is what you wanted! You didn't do your due diligence. I'm sorry, but it looks like this is going to cost you.

SOPHIA: I don't have the money.

TONY: Well, don't look at me. I'm tapped out.

SOPHIA: You can access more cash.

TONY: I am hyper-extended.

SOPHIA: But you have an enormous asset! Stonnington is earning money by just existing. You are literally a multimillionaire because you got into the Market before I was born.

TONY: You really don't know what you're talking about.

SOPHIA: I did everything you told me, I scrimped / and saved.

TONY: Save that shit for your mother. We have identified an actual problem. This is real life and now … We fix it.

SOPHIA: How?

TONY: I need some time to think.

SOPHIA: Oh!! So pleased I called you!

TONY: I can work this out. But this stays between us. Understand?

If your mother … If she ever hears about what I had to do to get you in here … I'm dead. She will … Okay? This stays in the vault.

SOPHIA: What have you done?

TONY: I did what I had to do in order to keep my family happy and safe.

SOPHIA: Okay Bruce Willis, but what the fuck does that mean?

*Beat.*

TONY: When I was a boy, my father beat me. He would lose a week's worth of wages on the horses and then he would drink and then he came home … And when I was fifteen years old I just started to stand in the doorway, you know? Like a nightwatchman. A silhouette. I knew it was me or my mother and … I learned how to take a punch. A good man makes the decisions for the family, and he takes responsibility when things go south. Being a good man is a lonely way to live a life. But my Julie … She deserves so much better.

TONY *is emotional,* SOPHIA *comforts him.*

SOPHIA: Dad, it's going to be okay.

TONY: I never said it wasn't.

SOPHIA: Nobody is perfect.

TONY: But don't you see, Kitten? … A bum like me … I ain't even close.

*There is silence. Then! Chaos!* GREG *bursts in, panting, and he screams when he finds* TONY *in the apartment,* TONY *screams also.*

Jesus! You scared the shit out of me.

GREG: Tony, Tony, Tony, I'm so sorry. Wow. Madonna and child … I'm so … sweaty. How was Elton?

TONY: What kind of person goes running at one o'clock in the morning?

GREG: It wasn't that late when I started. [*Showing his phone*] Thirty-nine-point-six kilometres. A circle. Twenty-five times around the fertiliser factory. There is literally nowhere to run to. You've been drinking. Is this about the crack?

TONY: / No.

SOPHIA: Yes.

> *Beat.*

/ No.

TONY: Yes.

SOPHIA: Nothing to worry about. Perfectly normal.

GREG: Oh great. I feel so reassured.

SOPHIA: Slabs crack all the time.

GREG: Yes, of course, so why is your father here at one in the morning?

SOPHIA: He left his laptop here.

GREG: What laptop?

SOPHIA: It's a funny story about the laptop actually.

GREG: You're lying.

SOPHIA: No, I'm not.

TONY: Yes we are!

SOPHIA: Dad.

TONY: Geoff is a good man. / Greg!

SOPHIA: Greg!

TONY: A fiancée deserves to know the truth. I'm not going to piss on your shoes and tell you it's raining.

GREG: That's good, because last time you did that it was a real mess.

TONY: Greg. Listen to me. Listen. Are you listening? Greg. You have cancer.

GREG: I have what?

TONY: But don't worry. You're not alone. The family is riddled with the shit.

GREG: How long have we got?

SOPHIA: A few months at most.

GREG: You're not joking.

SOPHIA: Nope.

GREG: What kind of cancer? Testicular, lung, a bowel?

SOPHIA: Concrete.

> SOPHIA *shows* GREG *the phone.*

TONY: Concrete cancer, Greg.

SOPHIA: The worst!

TONY: —Outside the Builders Warranty.

SOPHIA: So, the apartment is no longer covered by that insurance.

GREG: Holy shit, that's such a relief.

SOPHIA: A relief? / That's crazy talk, goddamnit.

TONY: It's a fucking disaster.

GREG: You said we all had cancer.

TONY: We do.

GREG: But we're not going to die. Right? It's concrete. It's a structural problem. It can be fixed. So, what are you going to you do?

TONY: I think you mean what are 'we' going to do.

GREG: We … ?

SOPHIA: Yes. 'We'.

GREG: *You* signed the papers. You both made this decision without me.

TONY: But you are getting married.

GREG: / Wait a second.

TONY: / So you are marrying into fifty percent of the problem.

SOPHIA: We are going to need to find more money to fix this.

> *Beat.*

GREG: Sorry. Am I getting fucked over?

Because it really feels like I am getting fucked here.

TONY: I am not fucking you, Greg.

GREG: It feels like you're trying to fuck me Tony!

TONY: You would know if I was trying to do that!

SOPHIA: The cancer is fucking all of us.

TONY: Just take it like a man!

> *Beat.* GREG *laughs too much.*

SOPHIA: You are laughing too long, too much.

GREG: I have worked like a dog!

TONY: Join the club!

GREG: I cannot afford to lose what I've got!

SOPHIA: Nobody can afford to lose, Greg!

GREG: You're not going to lose! You're golden.

> *He starts peeling off his clothes—he's having a panic attack.*

You've got a family. You are surrounded.
> They bailed you in, they will bail you out!
> I'm the only one here with my dick in my hand.

SOPHIA: I thought you were tougher than this.

GREG: You don't even know who I am!

TONY: You're the guy who proposed to my daughter.

GREG: Guess what Tony?

SOPHIA: Greg!

GREG: It's a funny story about us getting / married.

SOPHIA: Do not!

GREG: I think your father deserves the truth!

SOPHIA: You wanted in, I got you in! Two bedrooms and a cage full of debt.

GREG: Families are supposed to help each other.

SOPHIA: You want me to smile more too?

GREG: Two little words. Thank. You. You couldn't even say 'thank you'! Normal people say thank you for massive acts of generosity.

SOPHIA: I'm going out to score.

GREG: Congratulations!

SOPHIA: Fuck you Geoff! This is me.

GREG: So get on out there. Don't have to tell the whole world about it.

SOPHIA: I must reveal it to heal it.

TONY: What are you talking about?

SOPHIA: That's what I learned in Rehab.

TONY: So you're going out there to score some shit to deal with this problem.

SOPHIA: Yes.

TONY: Okay.

SOPHIA: You're not going to stand in the doorway and fight me?

TONY: Sophia. You always get what you want.

> *Silence.*

SOPHIA: Okay. I am the problem.

TONY: I never said that.

SOPHIA: Panicking about money and arguing with 'my husband' …

I cannot empathise, I cannot say thank you! Oh my god! I am turning into my mother!

TONY: I forbid you from doing that! Two of you is out of the question!

GREG *is genuinely freaking out now.* SOPHIA *rushes to hold him.*

SOPHIA: It's okay … Hey, hey … Okay. Listen … It's going to be okay.

GREG: I am not designed for this! I gave you everything I have and now I will be out on the street, under a cardboard box and I can't do that again! Pretending to be your fiancé is the biggest mistake of my life.

SOPHIA: We can fix it.

GREG: How do you fix a fake engagement?

TONY: Sophia?

SOPHIA: [*to* GREG] You're not going to die empty-handed.

TONY: What's he talking about, 'fake engagement'?

SOPHIA: We don't have rings.

TONY: He's freaking out!

SOPHIA: He is having a nervous breakdown.

TONY: He's not the only one! You told me you two made a commitment!

SOPHIA: We did! We made an agreement / and—

GREG: I cannot / continue to live like this.

TONY: I thought you were in / love!

SOPHIA: Everybody just shut the fuck up for a second! It is a problem! We can fix it.

SOPHIA *takes* GREG*'s hand.*

Greg …

SOPHIA *drops to both knees.*

You will make me the happiest person in the world Greg, if you do me the honour of … Will you marry me?

*Pause.*

TONY: Do I get an answer?

GREG: You had me at 'you're not going to die empty-handed'.

SOPHIA *and* GREG *embrace. The sound of a crack.*

*Door bursts open—*JULIE*!*

JULIE: I am not a fucking poodle!

TONY: Darling.

JULIE: Don't you 'darling' me, I have been waiting in that car for an hour!

This neighbourhood is crawling with gangbangers, meth-heads and high court judges. Did you get your laptop, Tony?

TONY: I must have left it at work.

JULIE: Jesus, Sophia. Your crack is enormous.

GREG: It's a cancer.

JULIE: It's what?

TONY: It's nothing to worry about.

JULIE: What are you talking about, nothing to worry about? Concrete cancer costs a fortune.

TONY: But this is the good kind of cancer.

JULIE: Tony. There is no *good* concrete cancer.

TONY: Well, Sophia was just / on the internet and—

SOPHIA: You would be amazed what I found out.

JULIE: You are both lying through your teeth.

SOPHIA: / Not completely.

TONY: Not this time …

> JULIE *examines the crack.*

JULIE: Show me the engineer's report.

> *Beat.*

I said, show me the report.

TONY: Funny story about that report …

JULIE: / Oh my god.

SOPHIA: There was some confusion about who was responsible for it.

JULIE: It's like talking to the Three Stooges!

GREG: But there's two of them—

JULIE: Welcome to the family.

TONY: This crack looks bad, but I have experience in mud / bricks and—

JULIE: Are you honestly going there, now?!

TONY: We have to be self-sufficient! We don't have the money to get a professional.

> *We hear a crack.*

JULIE: Michael is a Bitcoin zillionaire, surely he can help us.

TONY: He lost everything in the crash.

JULIE: I don't believe that for a second.

TONY: It's true. The Bitcoin price dropped fifty percent in two days Julie.

JULIE: How do you know the price dropped so fast?

*Beat.*

Tony. Oh my god. How much did you lose?
How much did you lose on Bitcoin?

*Loud sound of crack, nobody can deny it. This is tectonic-plates stuff.*

TONY: When we got married, we had nothing.

JULIE: Don't distract me. / Honestly. You're embarrassing yourself.

TONY: When did we decide we *had to have* a Miele kitchen? Polished concrete bench tops? Excess is everywhere!

JULIE: Just give me a straight fucking answer.

TONY: I am a problem solver.

JULIE: You look like a rasher of bacon.

TONY: No, I don't.

GREG: You kinda do.

JULIE: Tell me what you are not telling me!

TONY: I told you everything.

JULIE: I do not believe that.

TONY: Alright! God!

*Beat.*

But it's no big deal.

JULIE: Tell me!

TONY: I got us a reverse mortgage.

JULIE: No. You did not.

TONY: I did. On Stonnington.

JULIE: A reverse fucking mortgage …

TONY: It's a banking product.

JULIE: I know what it fucking is, Tony! Tell me you did not do this.

TONY: It seemed like a good idea.

JULIE: Not without my consent.

TONY: I think I can still fix this.

JULIE: I'm gonna put that on your tombstone!

TONY: We needed liquidity to pay for your mother. I thought she was going to be dead by now! That facility is like a front for the Mob.

Aqua-aerobics are fucking expensive and then *you* decided to go into politics and Sophia … I promised dollar-for-dollar for the deposit and … Transfer fees and taxes and now—the virus. Bitcoin. And the borders … so … we have run out of money.

*Beat.*

JULIE: But you thought it was a good idea at the time.

TONY: Our daughter needed us.

JULIE: Stop.

TONY: Can I just say—

JULIE *raises her hand. Silence.*

JULIE: Okay. Warren Buffet … What is the plan from here?

TONY: Plenty of other people have done this.

JULIE: —I am not going back to Gippsland again.

TONY: Gippsland was / a—

JULIE: A fucking catastrophe. Everything I ever earned sucked into that clusterfuck. A mud brick cottage, what / were you thinking?

TONY: Everybody was doing it.

JULIE: You made enormous frames for outrageous bricks, and you didn't read the instructions! That night we drove back to Carlton listening to Simon and Garfunkel singing 'America' … And do you remember what you said to me?

TONY: I think you're missing the point—

JULIE: *What* did you say to me Tony?

TONY: 'Everything is going to be okay'?

JULIE: No. You said: 'I don't know what comes first. The foundations or the walls.'

*Beat.*

You got the land, the wife, the kid. But no idea how to build the house. And so what did I do? Did I leave you? Did I sue you?

TONY: No.

JULIE: No! I gave you a handjob in the car and I told you.

'Everything is going to be okay.'

SOPHIA: Where was I while the handjob was happening?

JULIE: You were in the booster seat. Singing along with 'America'!

    *Pause.*

GREG: You can't stop here. I want to know what happened.

JULIE: Well, strap yourself on, Greg! Here we go! While the bricks are drying in Gippsland, I go to the Doomed Reading Room in the State Library, and I forensically research every book ever written on architecture and design.

SOPHIA: Maybe a *slight* exaggeration.

JULIE: Do not *try* to cancel me, Sophia! This happened. For me. My truth!

    Under the Doom I go deep into deconstructivism and meta-structural conventions. Fabrication, façade and fenestration, I breathe in Gehry and dream in Zara Hadid. By the end of the summer I have manufactured a new version of me. Self-controlled, self-assured, self—educated. Me at my best. And then. We return to Gippsland. To break out your father's bricks. I am mentally equipped to create our future but when we get there …

GREG: Oh no.

JULIE: That's right, Greg. His mud bricks degenerated.

GREG: Frames were too / big.

JULIE: Too big! Straw and grit and shit, just blowin' in the wind. Our plot, strewn with waste and we have nothing but the sand in our eyes.

GREG: / Wow.

JULIE: *This* was the first time I lost everything. So, Tony. Tell me. In your professional opinion. How fucked are we this time?

    *Beat.*

TONY: We are aspiring to be poor.

JULIE: Okay. I want a divorce. / Split the assets.

SOPHIA: You're never going to do that.

TONY: You are not a financial / expert.

JULIE: And *you* are not a banker, in Chelsea.

SOPHIA: That is low.

TONY: If we sell everything we own, it still won't even *begin* to clear our debt. We end up with less than what we started with. If we spilt up, we're out on the street.

JULIE: So, what will you take now? The gold in my teeth? Rings off my fingers? Saw off the whole hand. Put it in a pawn shop?

*Pause.*

You're supposed to say 'no' to that.

TONY: Best worst option … We move out of Stonnington. Do a long-term rental of the property. Use that cash flow to service the bank, when the borders open up and the travel industry gets back into business we may be able to get back on our feet. Or … with a bit of luck …

SOPHIA: With a bit of luck what?

TONY: Maybe your nonna might die. But that's a long shot.

JULIE: She's so healthy you could carve her.

*Beat.*

We were *this close* to the finish line … I touched it in my dreams. Tony. I can never forgive you.

GREG: I don't blame you.

JULIE: Thank you Greg. So. Now. Do we just go out there and join the gangbangers and the meth-heads? Where are we going to live?

TONY: Way I see it? … We only have one option.

TONY *and* JULIE *look to* SOPHIA *and* GREG … *it dawns on them.*

SOPHIA: Oh!! / No fucking way!

GREG: You have got to be joking!

JULIE: Congratulations!

*Lights snap out. Music comes up: 'Mess Around', Ray Charles.*

INTERVAL!

*DURING INTERVAL*

*In the outside world, things are getting worse. There are only four reasons for Victorians to leave their home: food and supplies, medical care and care giving, exercise, and work or education. Police have strong powers to enforce these directions and can issue on the spot fines, including up to $1,652 for individuals and up to $9,913 for businesses. Under the State of Emergency people who don't comply could also be taken to court and receive a fine of up to $20,000. Companies face fines of up to $100,000.*

*As I remember, this is actually true. I mean I was there so this is my lived experience through the fog of memory, baby.*

# ACT TWO

---

*SCENE ONE: SIX WEEKS LATER—NEW NORMAL*

*Darkness, thunder, whale music ... More thunder!*

SOPHIA *in a doorway, lit by the phone.*

SOPHIA: This is a funny story. You are going ...

> SOPHIA *begins to laugh.*

Okay ... Imagine you can only leave your home for food and medicine. Exercise, work or education. If the police catch you out there for any other reason, you can be arrested and fined twenty thousand dollars.

> *She stops laughing.*

Welcome to the Australian dream. A fissure in Maslow's Pyramid of Needs. But if you gaze long enough into an abyss, the abyss will gaze back into you.

> *In the darkness,* TONY *is playing Xbox.*

TONY: [*singing alone to the melody of 'Guantanamera'*] One Wayne Rooney! There's only one Wayne Rooooo-ney!

> One Wayne Roooo-ney! There's only one Wayne Roo—ne-y!

> *Beat.*

We need another Wayne Rooney!

> *Beat.*

Come on you Reds!

> TONY *continues while lights up slowly on the apartment overwhelmed with boxes and furniture. Tony and Julie have moved their whole house into this two-bedroom apartment and the crack in the floor is so wide now, it has hazard tape and witches' hats to alert people. You really need to step broadly across the gap in the floor. The walls are covered in Julie's self-portraits, Greg's work, and posters of Manchester United footballers.* TONY *is alone playing Xbox.*

I can make this work. *We can* ... Come on! Around him, steps inside and ... Yes! Julie? Have a look at this one. He shoots he scores!

> SOPHIA *enters from her bedroom, dressed for work and disappointed.*

[*At the game*] Red card?! ... No! This referee is screwing us over!
SOPHIA: Dad.
TONY: [*to* SOPHIA] Come on you Reds!
SOPHIA: It's too early.
TONY: Practice makes perfect.
SOPHIA: Greg won't be happy.

> JULIE *enters carting a huge painting of herself.*

TONY: Greg's out getting 'essential' coffees. And I am slaughtering PSG! Alone.
JULIE: [*to* SOPHIA] What are you looking at?
SOPHIA: Another self-portrait?
JULIE: I am examinationing the human condition.
SOPHIA: Looks painful.
JULIE: Such is life. [*To* TONY] If I entered this selfie in the Archie, would you longlist it?
TONY: In a New York minute.
JULIE: I am really reaching deep inside.
TONY: I can see that, baby.
JULIE: 'Thoughts are the shadows of our feelings—always darker, emptier and simpler.' Now. Sophia. You need to be here between ten a.m. and ten p.m..
SOPHIA: No. I have to get to work, I have two families arriving. And then I have to be at the facility for Nonna, she is having her assessment and ... you're not even listening are you?
JULIE: I can't believe you lied to me about quitting your job.
SOPHIA: I thought it was the smart thing to do at the time.
JULIE: Sophia, you're such a liar. You have to stay put in this apartment.
SOPHIA: Why do I have to be here?
JULIE: We are expecting a delivery.
TONY: Hallelujah! Baby! We just won the Euro Cup!
       Here we—go! / Here we go, here we go!
SOPHIA: Dad, can you please shut the fuck up / for a second?

JULIE: Don't speak to your father like that.

SOPHIA: No more deliveries Julie! There is *no* more space. No more.

JULIE: Just a teeny weeny little fairy bit of / space!

SOPHIA: Zero! Nought! Nijinsky! Your whole lives have been stacked into boxes. Clothes and books and garden tools! Lego, Meccano, Scalextric, surfboards, wetsuits, VHS and Beta, LPs, CDs, cassettes and a silver-service cutlery set, a couch and a dining-room table. Turkish rugs! An electric sitar, backpacks and bongs, and every baby picture, every souvenir, every piece of underwear you have ever owned and soiled, and an extensive selection of vibrators.

JULIE: For my neck. I have a condition …

SOPHIA: You don't need any more stuff!

TONY: We need our ten-piece Indonesian hardwood outdoor setting.

SOPHIA: Forget it! Chuck it! Leave it on the street!

JULIE: It comes in pieces, it will fit through the doorway!

SOPHIA: Sell it! We need the money! Nonna is bleeding us dry!

TONY: I built it with my own two hands. Indonesian rainforest. Hard. Wood.

SOPHIA: We literally have nowhere to put a hardwood setting.

JULIE: It's an outdoor setting, put it outdoors!

SOPHIA: Funny story about that! We don't have outdoors!
     We don't even have a balcony.

TONY: See! That little flat in South Yarra had a balcony. / Patio terrace thing.

SOPHIA: Every time I come into this room I want to rip you limb from limb!

JULIE: Sounds like you're pregnant.

SOPHIA: What?!

JULIE: Are you up the duff?

SOPHIA: No!

TONY: You're very grumpy in / the morning.

JULIE: Grumpy Sophia: explains a lot.

SOPHIA: I am not fucking pregnant!

JULIE: Take a test, make sure.

SOPHIA: Do not mimic me.

JULIE: That wasn't a mimic.

SOPHIA: You were gonna do it!

JULIE: No, I wasn't.

SOPHIA: / I know how your mind works! I know you.

JULIE: I wasn't mimicking anybody … 'I know you'.

SOPHIA: See? See? See? She did it! / You did it!

JULIE: That's not a mimic! That's just repeating whatever you say.

SOPHIA: Well, don't repeat whatever I say!

JULIE: Well, don't repeat what *I* say!

SOPHIA: I'm not, I don't.

JULIE: You do it all the time!

SOPHIA: *You* do all the time!

JULIE: / You're doing it now!

SOPHIA: You're doing it now!

JULIE: She's totally pregnant.

SOPHIA: What the fuck is wrong with you?

JULIE: I am an artist! Trying to survive under an oppressive far right regime!

SOPHIA: You signed a contract about acceptable behaviour. Bullet point three specifically references 'mimicry' and 'sarcastic tone'. Do I to have to read it again, to remind you?

JULIE: [*to* TONY] Got her period.

SOPHIA *grabs the written agreement and reads out loud.*

SOPHIA: 'No mimicking under any circumstances'! Bullet point three!

JULIE: [*mimicking*] 'Bullet point three!'

SOPHIA: You are here on a temporary visa!

JULIE: You wanna hit me don't you! You wanna punch me in the throat!

SOPHIA: I am going to pretend you didn't say that.

JULIE: Your father and I have possessions, and that is nine-tenths of the law.

TONY: We have a right to collect a life. At our age, if we don't have a house with surfboards and Turkish rugs and ten-piece settings, then what the hell have we been doing for the last fifty years? If our bodies were vaporised in a terrorist attack right now. Without all this shit in these boxes? How the hell will anybody know that we had been alive?

Nobody would know we even existed!

SOPHIA: The world doesn't need to know you existed.

TONY: I created a home for you.

SOPHIA: *That* is fucking hilarious! Mum was going to leave you!

JULIE: / That's enough! Sophia. Stop it.

TONY: That's a lie. That's a fairy tale!

SOPHIA: Do not try to rewrite my story. You used to brush my hair and help me get to sleep! … Now. You two deserve each other! I have to meditate!

> SOPHIA *puts on some whale music, composes herself, then.*

TONY: This whale music sucks ass.

JULIE: Whales sound retarded.

SOPHIA: I can hear you.

TONY: I am allowed to have an opinion on your whale music.

SOPHIA: This is my home, you are in my space.

JULIE: We live here too!

SOPHIA: Oh yeah! I forgot that for single moment in time!

> *Music continues—*SOPHIA *tries to meditate.*

JULIE: [*to* TONY] So, I was looking at the GoFundMe account and there's like three grand there. It's not a lot of money, but I was / thinking …

SOPHIA: I cannot believe I am hearing this.

JULIE: Stop eavesdropping.

SOPHIA: I did not create the GoFundMe for your personal expenses.

JULIE: Sophia, this is a private conversation.

SOPHIA: As the social media manager for Strap On Stonnington— I forbid you from using that account for personal use! I will not be part of this ethical and moral corruption!

JULIE: It is called GoFund*Me*. Not *Go let my daughter decide what to spend the money on.*

SOPHIA: I was raised to know the difference between right and wrong!

TONY: You're not the boss of us!

SOPHIA: Go to your room!

JULIE: Sophia!

SOPHIA: That bedroom is a pigsty! Get in there and clean it! And while you're cleaning it, take a good look in the mirror. Is this the person you want to be when you grew up?

TONY: How do you know it's a pigsty?

SOPHIA: Because I crawled in there yesterday!

JULIE: What are you doing crawling into our room?

SOPHIA: Don't you worry about what I was doing in there!

TONY: *So* not cool.

> JULIE *starts eating ice cream straight from the container.*

SOPHIA: You wanna know what's so not cool Tony? Rotting food behind the bed. Soggy cannoli and sausage rolls. That shit attracts rats! [*To* JULIE] Put that ice cream back immediately!

JULIE: I'm hungry!

SOPHIA: I don't care if you starve to death! You will not be eating ice cream for breakfast under my roof!

TONY: Answer the question! Why are you snooping around under the bed?!

SOPHIA: Because I am the maid who patrols the buffer zone between hygiene and your dripping prophylactics!

JULIE: [*laughing*] I told ya she was gonna find that franger!

SOPHIA: Why are you even bothering to use them? You don't have to worry about birth control.

JULIE: I don't want your father's spoof stains on my good sheets. Your nonna gave us those for Christmas.

TONY: Nobody said you could pick through our stuff.

SOPHIA: I cannot move without tripping over your stuff!

JULIE: I bet she was looking for porn.

SOPHIA: I was not looking for my father's pornographic magazine collection.

TONY: Well, you wouldn't have found anything under that bed.

JULIE: No. He keeps all that shit on his phone now.

TONY: That's not true! / Don't make up stuff like that. That's not fair.

JULIE: Saving the Amazon rainforest, one cumshot at a time.

SOPHIA: Enough! … The pair of you! … Stop!

> TONY *starts playing FIFA. The soccer game commentary underscores the scene.* JULIE *is painting her self-portrait.* SOPHIA *watches.*

You are not my children. You are my biological parents. Grow the fuck up. Stop morphing into difficult teenagers. I forbid you! Julie, what the fuck are you doing with your life?

JULIE: [*re: the painting*] This is my soul. In mixed-media on canvas. I call / it …
SOPHIA: Go out there and get a job!

> *Beat.*

JULIE: What did you just say to me?
SOPHIA: Nothing. I have to work.
JULIE: Can you stop at the shops on the way home?
SOPHIA: I'm not buying any more ice cream.
JULIE: You are fat-shaming me again!
SOPHIA: / Okay, okay …
JULIE: That is bullet point six. / 'No more fat-shaming'!
TONY: 'No more fat-shaming!'
SOPHIA: What do you want me to get?
JULIE: Banana and lemon.
SOPHIA: That's not a flavour.
TONY: [*re: the game*] Come on you Reds!!
JULIE: Get the Neapolitan and I'll mix it up with a mandarin.
SOPHIA: And what do you say?

> *Pause.*

What do you say, Julie?
JULIE: Please.
SOPHIA: And? …
JULIE: Congratulations.

> JULIE *continues painting herself, and* TONY *continues on FIFA.*

SOPHIA: I breathe like a humpback breaching. As a child, my mother promised I could choose the colour of my walls. What would be the outcome if she had fled Tony when she had the chance?
JULIE: [*to* SOPHIA] Are you still here?
SOPHIA: Sometimes people don't want to hear the truth because they don't want their illusions destroyed.

> SOPHIA *exits to get dressed.*

TONY: Sophia?
SOPHIA: [*off*] I am changing!
TONY: Tom Hanks got the China virus.
SOPHIA: [*off*] COVID-19.

JULIE: His wife got it too. / It's not all about Tom. Women have a right to get China virus as well! Soooo fucking misogynist.

TONY: Sophia, what is Tom Hanks' wife's name?

SOPHIA: [*off*] Stop yelling! Stop yelling at me!

TONY: [*re: the game*] Wayne Rooney! You weepy prick!

SOPHIA: [*off*] We have talked about your language!

JULIE: He's getting better.

TONY: These graphics are so realistic. If we get an account, for this, I can go online and play Rupert in London, in real time. [*To* SOPHIA] Hey Sophia! Have you got an online account for the Xbox?

JULIE: Sophia! Your father needs the code so he can play online with Rupert.

SOPHIA *storms in, wearing cool cotton pants and linen shirt.*

TONY: What's the code Sophia?!

SOPHIA: Stop yelling! At me! I am literally three feet away!

JULIE: You're not going out dressed like that.

SOPHIA: Yes, I am!

JULIE: You look like a priest at a youth camp.

TONY: [*re: the game*] Mother! Fucker!

SOPHIA: When are you leaving?!

TONY: Ohh, that's a whole conversation.

JULIE: What are you doing about the concrete cancer?

SOPHIA: I dunno, *what are we* going to do about the concrete cancer?

JULIE: So, now it's 'we'?

SOPHIA: Yes!

TONY: [*re: the game*] Fuck you Rooney! Pack your bags you ball slut!

SOPHIA: I am banning you from screaming 'slut' in my home!

TONY: But he never passes the ball! He hangs on until it's too late and—bam!

SOPHIA: It's a computer! You control his actions.

TONY: So why is he playing like such a cunt?

SOPHIA: Dad! I have neighbours!

TONY: They can't even speak English.

SOPHIA: That's it!

SOPHIA *rips the power cord from the wall.*

TONY: NO!!! … / Oh fuck man … what the fuck?

JULIE: Your father is playing Phifer!

SOPHIA: Nobody uses the c-word in this house, ever again.

JULIE: The c-word?

SOPHIA: The c-word.

JULIE: 'Congratulations'?

SOPHIA: That is not the word, and you know it.

JULIE: So, what is the word we're not allowed to say? … What is it?

SOPHIA: I'm not going to say it.

JULIE: How do we know what word you mean if you're not going to say it?

SOPHIA: [*mimicking*] 'How do we know, if you're not going to say it?'

JULIE: [*to* TONY] Did you hear what she said to me? Tony? … Say something! You look like a cardboard box!

TONY: Sophia.

SOPHIA: What?

TONY: You lost my whole career.

SOPHIA: No, *you did that* all by yourself when you acted like a dick in the emergency meeting! That is why you are an unemployed travel agent.

TONY: The travel industry is dead to me! I am talking about FIFA 16 … Manchester United! On the brink of Euro success! I could have become a professional gamer, but no! You had to pull the plug on my dreams.

JULIE: She's just an idiot.

TONY: A real der-head.

JULIE *and* TONY *mutter together we can hear.*

JULIE: Rupert …

…

TONY: Homosexual.

…

JULIE: Orgasm.

…

TONY: Boring.

JULIE: Frigid.

*They smile at* SOPHIA *and can only just stop themselves laughing.*

SOPHIA: Don't even try to gaslight me.

JULIE: Only a crazy person thinks they are being gaslit.

> *Silence—*SOPHIA *looks at the scene. Her father trying to reconnect the Xbox and her mother sneaking ice cream and painting a self-portrait.*

Wha? I'm not doin' nothin'.

SOPHIA: Just … wash the tub out when you're finished.

> SOPHIA *starts to leave.*

JULIE: You need to find some money to pay a structural engineer.

TONY: A structural engineer is going to charge a fortune.

JULIE: Maybe a second job.

TONY: Greg too.

JULIE: Yeah, Greg too.

TONY: He's doin' Nietzsche with this life.

> TONY *screams! He is getting electrocuted! Bam! Chaos! Screaming!* SOPHIA *and* JULIE *runs to his aid, as* GREG *appears in the doorway in running gear and a tray of coffee for everybody. He speaks fiercely, as if he has returned from Mount Everest.*

GREG: I would have been here sooner, but there is a ten-piece garden setting smashed to pieces in the middle of the road, some guy's just dumped it and a truck ran right into it. Shit is everywhere. Man. A good barista is an essential worker! The real pandemic heroes! Long black, skinny flat white with caramel and a marshmallow for Julie. It smells in here. What is that?

SOPHIA: My father is on fire.

GREG: Hey! Tony? Put it away. No Xbox before ten a.m., champ! Bullet point fifteen. Here's your hot chocolate with triple cream.

> TONY *takes his coffee, shaking.*

Hold it like a man! What's the matter, are you on drugs?

SOPHIA: He electrocuted himself.

JULIE: [*re: the coffee*] Too much caramel. Take it back.

SOPHIA: Don't be ungrateful.

JULIE: Tastes like camel poo.

SOPHIA: You don't know what camel poo tastes like.

JULIE: Take it back!

GREG: Okay, okay.

SOPHIA: You're not going back to 'Nancy's'.

GREG: She won't drink it.

SOPHIA: Not the point.

JULIE: That coffee is camel shit and I'm not going to drink it.

GREG: I'll get you another one, Kitten.

SOPHIA: What?

GREG: I'll go back and get another one—

SOPHIA: For 'Kitten'?

JULIE: I am a pushing the boundaries. I need sustenance, Sophia.

SOPHIA: I'm going to push *your boundaries* in a minute.

JULIE: Are you still going to paint me Greg? You said you want to paint me, you know I / want you to paint me.

SOPHIA: [*to* GREG] She's got you wrapped around her little finger. You treat her like a princess! There is nothing wrong with that coffee!

GREG: Stop undermining me!

TONY: Person! Woman! Man!

GREG: Mother of fuck! Tony, what are you talking about?

TONY: I have just been electrocuted.

GREG: Yes! And? …

TONY: We are living in a disaster.

GREG: How so?—

> GREG *goes towards the kitchen, stepping over the crack.*

Go on, I'm listening.

JULIE: You need an engineer's report to mount a legal case.

GREG: [*calling out*] Three grand is a helluva lot of money for a family of four.

> GREG *enters with his coffee now in 'a proper cup'.*

SOPHIA: What's in the cup?

GREG: *My* coffee.

SOPHIA: You went to 'Nancy's' and bought takeaway coffee and now you're drinking that coffee out of a china cup?

GREG: Yeah.

SOPHIA: What'd you do with the paper cup?

GREG: Threw it away.

SOPHIA: Excuse me?

GREG: I threw it away.

SOPHIA: Just—tossed it?

GREG: I like my coffee in a proper coffee cup! What's the matter?

SOPHIA: Nothing.

GREG: Don't get all passive-aggressive. Just tell me.

SOPHIA: You really wanna know what is wrong?

GREG: Yes, I do!

SOPHIA: You are killing the planet!

GREG: Single-handedly?

SOPHIA: Yes!

GREG: It's just a cup!

SOPHIA: A single-fucking-use cup! Yes!

GREG: I am doing the planet a favour! I brought my coffee home and now I want to drink my coffee from a proper coffee cup! It's what I do.

SOPHIA: Oh! Goodie! It's what you do! So, let's all just live like kings and queens and eat ice cream and leave our frangers on the floor! The maid will clean up the mess! And the children of the poor people will live huddled on the edges of the world! Clinging together for life and cursing our names!

GREG: If you don't want your long black, just say so, I'll take it back and get you a double chai! Whatever will make you happy.

SOPHIA: It will make me happy if you go and get that paper cup out of the garbage and drink your coffee from it.

GREG: You want me to take this cup of coffee, go and get that single-use paper cup that I discarded after I used it … singularly … and pour this coffee into that disgusting single-use cup from the garbage and drink that coffee? That's what you want me to do?

SOPHIA: Yes. That is what I want Greg and don't you dare push me on this! Because after the morning I've had with these two? Right now? I am ready to rip out a spleen !

GREG: Happy wife, happy life.

> GREG *brings the paper cup back into the room. Makes a big deal about sipping the coffee from the paper cup he had discarded.*

There! We! Go! … Good java. 'Roasted on premises'. Yes! Look at me! Saving a planet with a single-use cup. So … satisfying.

TONY: Did you really get that cup out of the garbage?

JULIE: [*to* TONY] Shut up. Mummy and Daddy are fighting.

SOPHIA: Mummy and Daddy are not fucking fighting!

GREG: Feels like we're fighting to me!

SOPHIA: We are not their bloody parents!

GREG: Jesus, no!

JULIE: You have to admit—you fight a lot.

GREG: We never used to.

SOPHIA: No. And then you two came along. We used to have time for ourselves.

TONY: You used to play Xbox with me all the time.

SOPHIA: Well, that was then.

TONY: We used to talk about football together

SOPHIA: Yes. Because that is what *you* wanted! In reality, I do not care about Man United. I could not give two craps about Wayne Rooney! That was all an act to secure some attention as a child, hoping that you might take an interest in me and now … Now? … I am the only one in this family with a job. So that worked out well. My life. A blueprint for maleficence and addiction. Come on you Reds! For the sake of fuck.

> SOPHIA *storms into the bedroom. Pause.*

JULIE: That was weird what happened, with the cup.

GREG: As a maverick Independent what is your policy about paper cups?

JULIE: I …

> *She mumbles something inaudible.*

GREG: Speak up Julie, you're mumbling.

> JULIE *mumbles something inaudible.*

I SAID, WHAT IS YOUR POLICY ON PAPER CUPS?!

JULIE: I don't have a policy! Okay?! I don't have a policy on paper cups.

SOPHIA: [*off*] Why don't you have a policy on sustainable use of paper cups?

JULIE: You two are bullying me!

GREG: / NO! We're not! Why don't you have a policy position?

SOPHIA: [*off*] NO! We're not!

JULIE: Because I dropped out.

GREG: You did what? Why?

JULIE: It is hard enough to remember my opinions, without also remembering my reasons for them! So I quit.

GREG: You quit?

JULIE: You bet.

SOPHIA: [*off*] She what?

JULIE: Ohhh shit.

SOPHIA *enters slowly, she is brushing her own hair.*

SOPHIA: You didn't tell me you quit.

JULIE: Sophia … I thought you would be mad.

SOPHIA: Why would I be mad? … Julie? After I built you a kick-arse website with all your socials and a GoFundMe button? After I researched and authored actual policy platforms for you on immigration, health, education, climate and shared my contacts and told everybody I know to 'Vote One for the Strap-On!' And now you quit. Without a word to me. Why would you think I would be mad?

JULIE: I knew you / would be angry.

SOPHIA: I am not angry.

JULIE: You sound fucking angry!

SOPHIA: I am not angry! I am just … so disappointed.

*Beat*—JULIE *starts stabbing at the painting with her brush, while …*

I just want the best for you. Why is that so hard to understand? Honestly. Mum you have so much potential, but it makes me wonder what is going on in that little head?

JULIE: [*re: the portraits*] This! An empty loveless void. You never listen.

SOPHIA: / Not true! Don't play this game with me!

JULIE: You're always fighting. Everything is just too hard.

TONY: I don't believe you don't love football!

SOPHIA: [*to* TONY] Hey! Ronaldo! Not *everything* is all about you!

TONY: You treat your mother like a baby.

SOPHIA: I do not treat my mother like a baby! She is not a fucking baby.

JULIE: I am not a fucking baby.

SOPHIA: [*to* TONY] You're making her cry.

TONY: She started it!

SOPHIA: Grow up!

JULIE: Why is everybody being so mean to everybody?!

TONY: I'm not going to take responsibility for her being a baby!

JULIE: This is a horrible place to live!

SOPHIA: Alright! This is finished! I refuse to live like this!

GREG *is making loud whale noises! Trying to calm the fight.*

SOPHIA: [*to* GREG] What the fuck, dude?

GREG: To Zen us out.

GREG *makes more whale noises.*

TONY: Is that supposed to be a whale?

JULIE: Sounds like sperm to me.

JULIE *and* TONY *begin to snigger.*

GREG: Humpback. I choose to be a humpback whale.

TONY: Hump.

TONY *sniggers.*

GREG: If you care about Sophia, you know what you can do!

GREG *makes a loud whale noise.* JULIE *joins in making a whale noise with* GREG, *then* TONY *joins in and the three of them are making whale noise to try and calm* SOPHIA. *Their whale noises continue and crescendo until they reach a natural climax and then ... silence.*

SOPHIA: I found that surprisingly relaxing.

JULIE: It is actually fun to be a whale. I'm sorry you're losing your shit.

SOPHIA: Thank you Julie.

Everybody? ... This must stop. I do not want to hear another nasty word under this roof. No more fighting. With anybody. [*To* JULIE] Be kind and we can make it. One day at a time.

JULIE *gently places her head in* SOPHIA*'s lap.* SOPHIA *brushes* JULIE*'s hair. They hold this pose throughout the following.*

So much hurt, so many tears. So many feelings ... Weird, I know. Now. Together, we must do something about the elephant in the room.

*Pause*—JULIE, GREG *and* TONY *look at each other.*

The crack.

I am talking about the crack … for the sake of fuck … I'm not inferring there is an actual elephant … See? This is the problem we must address and then we can get back to our normal lives again.

Okay.

The structural engineer's report.

We can split it. Fifty-fifty.

GREG: Sounds good.

TONY: Great.

SOPHIA: You're happy.

TONY: Yes.

GREG: Compromise rocks.

JULIE: That's very kind of you, Sophia.

TONY: You two have got a great relationship.

*Beat.*

SOPHIA: What are you talking about?

JULIE: You said 'fifty-fifty'. You and Greg, sharing the costs together.

GREG: Fifty is you and fifty is us.

SOPHIA: *We* are sharing the costs / together.

TONY: Hang on a second.

GREG: You're not even paying us any rent. So, fifty-fifty. Okay?

JULIE: You already owe us more money than you can imagine.

GREG: You gave us that money.

JULIE: I don't remember anybody saying anything about a gift.

GREG: It was a gift.

TONY: No. No gift.

GREG: You gave us the money to help us get into the Market.

TONY: I didn't give *you* anything. I had never even met you.

SOPHIA: We measured this room together.

TONY: We had a deal.

SOPHIA: I was under the impression it was a gift.

JULIE: So why did you refuse to say 'thank you'?

*Beat.*

The night we went to the Elton John tribute show, we stood in this very room together, to celebrate the joint purchase of this property and you said the c-word. 'Congratulations.' That *is* what you said to us.

SOPHIA: So, we're playing this game, now?

TONY: We don't play games.

SOPHIA: Ohhh. 'No games'! Okay. So, if there was *no gift*—that makes us 'co-owners' and so then it makes *even more sense* that we *split* the engineering expenses fifty-fifty.

TONY: You are conflating the wrong ends of the stick.

JULIE: / That's not what this is about. No. I agree with your father.

GREG: No, / this is the discussion. We are having the same discussion.

SOPHIA: No, no, no. Dad. That's not how this works. This is the deal! /

GREG: You want 'in'? Okay! You are fucking 'in', old man.

TONY: Don't you call me 'old man' again.

GREG: What are you gonna do, cough on me?

SOPHIA: Fifty percent ownership buys you fifty percent of the expenses.

TONY: Your grandmother is bleeding us dry!

SOPHIA: Not my problem. You have to get out!

TONY: We have literally nowhere else to go!

SOPHIA: Why not?

JULIE: Your father has compromised our financial future to help you!

TONY: Everything we do, we do it for you!

JULIE: Family!

TONY: Flesh and blood. An investment in future generations.

GREG: Are you on drugs? Is everybody on drugs without me?

TONY: We are in a difficult position.

GREG: We need thousands of dollars immediately!

And I wanna be on drugs too!

TONY: I know Greg, and I didn't want to do this … But … you're forcing my hand.

> TONY *holds* JULIE*'s hand out to show the rings.*

Sophia, if you don't mind assuming the position?

JULIE: What are you doing?

> TONY *wraps* SOPHIA*'s arms around* JULIE*, then gets a good grip on* JULIE*'s ring finger.*

TONY: Since you won't let us access the GoFundMe Account, your mother has to take one for the team.

JULIE: / I have not agreed to any of this!

TONY: One, two, three! Heave! Take it easy baby!

*They begin trying to leverage the rings off* JULIE*'s fingers.*

[*To* JULIE] I think I have to put my knee on you somewhere.

SOPHIA: One! Two!

*They groan and moan until—*GREG *pulls the family apart.*

JULIE: Greg! He almost pulled my ring off!

GREG: Nobody acts like this in real life!

SOPHIA: This is my lived experience.

TONY: We need that ring!

GREG: Leave! Her ring! Alone!

JULIE: Thank you Greg.

GREG: [*to* TONY] Are you proud of yourself?

TONY: Greg, Stephan Hawking once said: 'Life is the survival of the fittest.'

GREG: No! *Stephen* Hawking did not say life is survival of the fittest! That was *Darwin* and he was looking at the planet through an outdated patriarchal-heteronormative-analysis of shit. Life is community. We cohabitate or we die alone.

TONY: I don't think so, Greg.

JULIE *and* TONY *put their shoes on. They begin to exit. It feels like this may be the last time we ever see them. They may never return ...*

SOPHIA: Dad ...

*They stop.*

Have you had any job offers? ...

TONY: No. Not a one.

SOPHIA: Keep on looking, there's gotta be something out there on the horizon.

TONY: Truth be told, there aint a whole lot out there, for an old man like me.

TONY *slips on leather jacket, holds hands with* JULIE.

GREG: You're leaving?

TONY: Yes Greg—

JULIE: We're getting ice cream.

*They smile and exit.*

SOPHIA: I don't say he's a great man.

GREG: No.

SOPHIA: My father never made a lot of money.

GREG: What?

SOPHIA: His name was never in the paper.

GREG: / What are you saying? … what?

SOPHIA: But he's a human being. So, attention must be paid to such a person.

GREG: Are we in a play? Because you people are talking like you're in a play.

SOPHIA: You're the one who has been pretending to be in love with me.

GREG: I am living my truth, okay? I am the only authentic voice in this apartment.

SOPHIA: You forced me to get engaged to you!

GREG: / I forced you? … I was not hysterical! … You made a choice!

SOPHIA: You were hysterical! You gave me no choice! I had to propose just to shut you up!

GREG: I did not make you do anything!

SOPHIA: I am surrounded by a household of gaslighters!

GREG: So what does that make us now?

SOPHIA: Complicit!

> *Beat.*

GREG: Sophia. I'm not going to lie. I don't know what the hell I'm doing.

> Sometimes I sit in this apartment, all alone.
>
> And I think of the mortgage I am paying. And it's crazy!
>
> But then, this is what I always wanted.
>
> An apartment, a bed, a cage. I got all that I wanted and still … Goddamnit. I am lonely.
>
> And I do not want to live the rest of my life in a domestic tragedy.

SOPHIA: Cool.

GREG: Cool?

SOPHIA: Me too.

GREG: Okay. We have to get real, because look at us—we are miserable!

SOPHIA: I know, but hetero marriage has nothing to do with happiness.

> It is a business decision, that's all. Look at my parents. They are

fucking mental. Nobody gets married and gets away with it. In another world? Another lifetime … But this is fucken it. We can't go on drifting on the raft of the Medusa. We're going to end up like them. Eating ice cream and having baby boomer sex.

GREG: That image is going to stay with me.

SOPHIA: How do we get out of this funk?

> *Pause.*

GREG: Do you know about Tom Hanks?

SOPHIA: Yeah, sure. I mean, not personally. But in the landscape of popular culture, sure. I am relatively familiar with Tom Hanks. Not as a *relative*, but … Why?

GREG: He's on the Gold Coast. He's got the virus.

SOPHIA: Tom Hanks is in Australia?

GREG: Yes. And this virus … Death is pretty common / now.

SOPHIA: Death is so hot right now, it is epic.

GREG: / I know, right?

SOPHIA: A lot of buzz around death.

GREG: So if death can happen to Tom Hanks, I mean, how old is Tom Hanks?

SOPHIA: Dunno, he looks way old. Adult children. Father. Actor. Chameleon.

GREG: My point is—Tom Hanks could be your parents.

SOPHIA: Oh, I would love that.

GREG: No. I mean … dead.

SOPHIA: Okay. What exactly is your point?

GREG: Safe space?

SOPHIA: Safe space.

GREG: Okay. So, we agree. Your parents are really annoying.

SOPHIA: Totally annoying.

GREG: So, maybe we have them killed?

> *Silence.*

Just an idea.

> *Pause.*

Terrible, terrible thing to say, I am so sorry Sophia. So sorry.

SOPHIA: Wait a second … Are you recording this conversation?

GREG: No, are you?

SOPHIA: Not yet.

GREG: Good. Because … that could really come back to bite me. If you were to turn State's Witness or something.

SOPHIA: I don't think we have 'State's Witness' / in Australia.

GREG: Short handing. Okay. So? … Thoughts, suggestions? Responses?

*Pause.*

SOPHIA: As the only daughter, for me—this conversation is—problematic.

GREG: Would you feel more comfortable if they were … included?

SOPHIA: I don't know. Is it possible that we can kill them … humanely?

GREG: Humanely. Would be—entirely possible. I would imagine.

*Pause.*

SOPHIA: I lost my shit about your coffee.

GREG: Yeah, that's okay.

SOPHIA: I'm not apologising. I'm revealing, to heal.

GREG: / Of course.

SOPHIA: / We are very different people.

GREG: Is this a break-up? Are you breaking up with me?

*Beat.*

Or … murdering with me?

SOPHIA: I don't want to live my life in debt, to a banker I have never met.

Maybe we just walk away from all this? Front-door key in the letterbox and just—vanish. Whoosh. Gone.

GREG: But this is what you wanted.

SOPHIA: No. Not this—is awful … / messy.

GREG: Yes … fucked up. But this is what you *told me* you wanted.

SOPHIA: I did not want to live with my parents. I wanted to own a property. Security. But I don't want the financial responsibility. This is bullshit. This is a rip off! I'm a zombie. Work, eat, shit, clean, work. No freedom, no control … I am turning into a maverick independent.

GREG: Do you still want Rupert? / Is that what this is about?

SOPHIA: No! Christ! You sound like Tony! / My life is not determined by—

GREG: Okay! Okay! What do you want Sophia?! / What do you want? Goddamnit. What the fuck do you want?!

SOPHIA: More! I want more. I need more! More! More!

GREG: More what?

SOPHIA: Freedom. To start again.

GREG: So, we agree. They have to die.

> *Pause.*

SOPHIA: You know, I just can't think of any other way out.

GREG: Okay.

SOPHIA: It's ironic. Because once? In this very room? My father made me promise …

> *Pause.*

Doesn't matter.

GREG: What did Tony make you promise Sophia?

SOPHIA: He forgets.

GREG: What did he make you promise?

> SOPHIA *laughs too long and too hard. Crack! Lights out.*

## SCENE TWO: AN HOUR LATER—THUNDER SCENE

*Lights up. The crack in the floor is wider.*

*JULIE and TONY arrive back in the apartment with plastic bags of canned food and armfuls of toilet paper.*

JULIE: Sophia! Your father just stole a shit-ton of pasta.

TONY: Everybody was grabbing it, so I just started throwing punches.

But we all love pasta right? We all got a little bit of Roman Empire in there somewhere.

> *Beat.*

It's quiet. Too quiet. [*Calling out*] Sophia!!

> *Thunder outside.*

SOPHIA: [*off*] We have to talk about what happened this morning.

TONY: What happened this morning?

SOPHIA: [*off*] The argument.  .

JULIE: What argument?

SOPHIA: [*off*] We had a family disagreement and Greg and I have decided how we want to move forward.

JULIE: What did you decide?

*SOPHIA enters wearing black latex gloves and carrying a clothesline cord which can be used for strangulation, she is testing it for strength.*

SOPHIA: We have some options on the table.

JULIE: So you speak about us behind our back?

*Thunder outside. GREG enters in apron and carrying a baseball bat.*

GREG: Back*s*.

TONY: You intentionally exclude your parents!

SOPHIA: Yes.

JULIE: But why?

GREG: Because we are discussing different ways to have you humanely killed and *that*—is a little 'sensitive'.

*Thunder outside.*

JULIE: See, this is something that Rupert would *never* do. Rupert never *makes jokes* about a murder plot—the way you just did. Because news flash! Murder is not very funny, Greg. Now, what were you really talking about behind our backs? The hygiene, the ten-piece outdoor setting? The franger?

*Pause.*

Fine! Play your silent games.

But you may be interested to know that before we left, I planted a listening device in the flowers.

*Thunder outside.*

And I intend to listen back to that recording and determine the truth for myself!

*Thunder outside.*

I'm only kidding. [*To* GREG] You should see your face.

TONY: Kitten. I think you may be on to something.

JULIE: What are you talking about?

TONY: Murder can be an act of love.

TONY *motions for thunder, but there is none.*

Okay. Yes. The first time we stood in this room …

*He takes the baseball bat.*

Sophia made me a promise.

JULIE: What promise?

GREG: Yes, what promise?

TONY: Do you remember the promise you made to me, Sophia?

SOPHIA: Of course I remember the promise!

TONY: Well! What are you waiting for?

*Beat.* TONY *and* SOPHIA *are standing nose to nose now.*

I thought we had a deal!

JULIE: / This is another deal? On top of the last one?

GREG: Another deal? That's a lot of deals.

TONY: Tell your mother Sophia! What did you agree to do?

SOPHIA: I agreed that I would murder my father!

*Thunder outside.*

JULIE: / Sophia!

GREG: You agreed?!

TONY: Yes! My only child! Agreed to murder me, for the financial benefit of the whole family.

TONY *motions for thunder, but there is none.*

This is with whom we are dealing with, whom, Julie. A young woman *so driven* to achieve property ownership that she is willing to take my innocent life. To murder me in my own cold blood. This is the child you suckled and raised from a babe! What do you think about that?

*Beat.*

JULIE: How come she gets to do the killing?

TONY: What?

*Thunder outside.*

JULIE: I wanna be the one to murder you Tony! I think I deserve it. Look at us. This isn't a life. We can't even have people over. We are mentally and socially retarded. You have life insurance. This is a great idea!

TONY: Yes, but …

*Thunder outside.*

Hang on a minute.

JULIE: It needs to look like natural causes …

SOPHIA: Then they pay up.

TONY: But honey …

JULIE: Or accidental death.

TONY: Yes. But … Honey, we are happily / married. With many years ahead of us, right?

JULIE: Yes, yes, yes of course, Tony.

*Beat.*

But you made a deal.

TONY: I was joking.

*Thunder outside.*

GREG: You made a deal Tony.

SOPHIA: A deal is a deal!

TONY: You're serious?

JULIE: How about—we walk up to the roof, and you just push him off?

SOPHIA: Too easy.

TONY: Wow.

SOPHIA: Okay let's go.

TONY: Wait a second, wait a second.

*He grabs onto the furniture.*

Jumping off the roof? Are you crazy?

JULIE: You're not actually jumping, it's a little push.

TONY: The roof has got 'suicide' written all over it.

JULIE: They don't pay out on suicide?

TONY: I'd need to check the policy. / But …

GREG: I've got it! Hit and run! We run you down / in a car!

JULIE: Great idea! The 'hit and run' is a classic.

TONY: You don't even own a car.

SOPHIA: We rent one.

GREG: A really big heavy one.

SOPHIA: With a big fucking bull bar!

TONY: Renting a car will leave a paper trail!

*Beat.*

JULIE: / That's a good point … Yeah. Yup.

SOPHIA: A good plan is all about those little details, isn't it?

> SOPHIA, JULIE *and* GREG *are thinking. Then …*

GREG: Food poison! / That's good. I can talk to some people.

SOPHIA: How about food poison?

TONY: No!

JULIE: What's wrong with poison?

TONY: I imagine it's very fucking agonising.

JULIE: Oh, poor baby …

TONY: This is my murder we're talking about; I demand the right to input.

> *Beat.*

SOPHIA: A train! / You get hit by a train!

GREG: That's good. A train is awesome.

TONY: Jesus, Sophia.

GREG: Great idea.

TONY: What a mess! The driver—the PTSD … no. I don't want my brains on his windshield for all eternity! No. I think we can all agree now … Murdering me is just silly.

SOPHIA: Well fuck, Dad. It was your idea.

TONY: It was silly.

JULIE: What happened to 'a deal's a deal'?

> *Thunder outside.*

TONY: Let's have ice cream. Who wants ice cream?

GREG: But it sounds like it's going to rain …

> JULIE, SOPHIA *and* GREG *are looking at* TONY *like they want to kill.*

TONY: Sweetheart. I know you love ice cream.

JULIE: It has to be something domestic.

SOPHIA: And logical.

GREG: Has to be logical.

SOPHIA: Got it! Drug overdose?

JULIE: Great idea!

TONY: I am not going to die like a / drug addict, Greg. No offence Sophia, but … How fucking dare you!

GREG: Mogadon asphyxiation.

SOPHIA: It's a pretty good suggestion …

JULIE: Plastic bag. Over the head. Suffocate on the vomit!

SOPHIA: / High-five Mum!

GREG: Fucking poetic!

JULIE: Pump him full of vodka to make sure he chunders!

GREG: Win, win, win, win.

TONY: Are you mental? A plastic bag and vodka?

JULIE: Keep your hair on!

TONY: It screams self-destruction!

SOPHIA: We're doing our best.

JULIE: It's like reeling in a whale.

GREG: Tony. Lemme ask you a question.

TONY: What is it?

GREG: Where do you stand on auto-erotica?

SOPHIA: Now, you're talking! Death by sexual misadventure!

JULIE: Going out with a bang *and* a whimper!

TONY: Can I just interject here … I *suggested* Sophia murder me, *to be polite*! So she would not be burdened by me in an aged-care facility. I thought I could trust you not to kill me prematurely.

But clearly, I was mistaken. Don't apologise all at once!

SOPHIA: We can go back to basics and electrocute you again.

JULIE: You've already done it once.

TONY: Yes! And it really fucking hurt!

*GREG starts writing in pencil on a piece of paper.*

SOPHIA: You always back out! This is what you do!

TONY: I wanna die in my sleep! Like my father.

Slip into the vapour. Sans suffering!

He was an arsehole all his life, didn't give two shits about his family. I have done everything humanly possible to keep you pricks happy and now I think I have earned the right to die of natural causes. What's wrong with that? I am a simple man with modest ambitions, that's all!

GREG: You put the *baby* in boomer!

*He hands paper to* TONY.

TONY: What's this?

GREG: Eviction! Both of you! Out!

TONY: You cannot throw your parents onto the street.

SOPHIA: We will not live like this any longer.

TONY: There are plenty of people who are worse off than you.

Think about the poor pricks in the City of Hume! Packed in like sardines. This is a mansion! Our first flat was a shoebox! A matchbox, no! A pinprick. We lived in a pinprick with no running water. No gas, no phone, no light. It was rezoned as a black hole. We had to split ourselves into atoms. We slept in a crack in the fabric of time! Living the Australian dream! But young people today just want everything handed to them on a plate.

GREG: This is family business. It's nothing personal.

TONY *opens the eviction notice.*

TONY: [*reading*] 'You are being evicted as of yesterday. There is nothing you can do. So don't even tie.' Don't even tie? / is that right? I don't get it. You don't want me to wear a 'tie'?

JULIE: Ha … / Well, that doesn't make any sense to me. 'don't tie' … ?

GREG: / No, that's 'try', don't even 'try.' It's pretty fucking obvious.

SOPHIA: That's just a detail. Don't get hung up on the typos. Don't even *try*.

GREG: 'Don't even try!'

TONY: Oh.. Don't even 'try'. Okay. So, there's more. [*Reading*] 'We are a generous open-hearted people; we have a proud record of welcoming people. But we will decide who comes to this apartment and the circumstances in which they come.'

GREG: That's right.

TONY: Okay. So, let me get this straight, Kitten.

SOPHIA: Knock yourself out.

TONY: My sperm gave you every opportunity that I could not afford …
I supported you through an expensive series of failures at university until you found your way to Rehab, and I paid for six months there and then I paid for you to requalify and go into the gold mine career of community development and then … you broke Rupert's heart and pretended to fall in love with, exhibit A …

*All* so you could convince me to give you more money than I could possibly afford to pay back to the bank, so that you can '*get into* the Market'.

SOPHIA: Yes … But does that make me a bad person?

GREG: 'Exhibit A' … ?

SOPHIA: None of us are bad people.

TONY: But when you spread all the details out like that—

SOPHIA: Yes?

JULIE: You do sound like a bit of cunt.

SOPHIA: Mum!

JULIE: We must reveal it to heal it. Darling.

SOPHIA: You two psychopaths have twisted my bowel.

JULIE: Another—sordid image.

SOPHIA: [*to* TONY] I know I am not the child you wanted. I know I don't make you happy. I know when I was born, somebody else was roaming in your imagination. A Rupert. A Geoff … a boy. But I did everything within my power … I lied and I cheated and I tried to please you. I renovated myself for you. But in my bones … I knew … This is it. And it will never be the best house on the worst street. I just don't have the chromosomes you wanted. And that is not my fault. This is who I am. I'm sorry … Greg. I am really sorry I dragged you into this. I hope you can forgive me because you're the closest thing I've got to a real friend. I love you, and I don't want to lose you because of my family.

JULIE: You had a perfect upbringing. The sacrifices I made for you.

SOPHIA: What sacrifice?

> JULIE *holds out her own engagement ring.*

JULIE: My. Life. Ever since you could speak you have lied to your parents. You lied about Greg. You lied for real estate!

GREG: From whom do you think she learned how to lie, from?

JULIE: She is a bad seed!

GREG: Julie! Your daughter learned to lie from you!

JULIE: / Oh—

GREG: It was a rhetorical question, you moron.

SOPHIA: Don't call my mother a moron.

GREG: You see! Look! The lesson!

> This is the lesson from the play you are living. In …
>
> There is more to a family than white-anting and gaslighting.

> *Pause.*

TONY: Is / there? Really?

JULIE: Is that a lesson? I don't think that's right.

GREG: Family is not a contest.

*They look at him—what is it?*

It is the map of the world we inhabit …
You know … Where we live, is our universe.

*Beat.*

SOPHIA: / That's pretty good.

JULIE: Not bad.

*Beat.*

TONY: Maybe the kid is right?

GREG: Well, I am the outsider. So. I'm here for that.

*Cracking noise.*

TONY: Sophia. I have to admit, I know nothing about real estate. Nothing, nada …

SOPHIA: Don't say it.

TONY: But being with you made me feel useful. The time we spent—okay—maybe I was selfish? But to me it was a simple act of …

JULIE: Deception.

TONY: When you put it that way. [*To* GREG *and* SOPHIA] Look, you *crazy kids* … I don't know if you are in love or … Who knows? Who cares? In the end, what is life? You play the game. Grow your hair. Pick up an investment property in the recession. What can I tell ya? Capitalism is kooky. Every man for himself and ne'er the less! 'Twas an honest mistake and now? … Now we must do the honourable thing.

SOPHIA: You're raiding the GoFundMe account?

TONY: No Kitten. My wife and I will take our departure and live out our remaining declining years on the street, where you live. Surviving on Ethiopian goat boxes. We may see you out there, on the street where we will live.

SOPHIA: Are you really leaving this time?

TONY: Yes. Sophia, you finally got what you wanted.

SOPHIA: Bullshit.

TONY: / Bullshit?

SOPHIA: Bull—shit! Yes! That is horsey, hairy bullshit!

> Tony. Two bedrooms, a cage and a husband.
>
> You forced me in! This is what you wanted me to want.
>
> … No offence Greg, but you know what I / mean.

GREG: Yeah, I get it. / Totally.

SOPHIA: And now! Every night! I am haunted by the thunder of my overwhelming debt. I cannot sleep! Your dream is suffocating me but it didn't have to be this way! Julie? What would have happened if you had saved us when you had the chance …

JULIE: Sophia …

SOPHIA: All those years ago. That semi-detached in Brunswick.

> What would have happened if we had got *out* instead of in.
>
> If we looked after each other just a little bit..
>
> What colour would our walls be now?

> *Pause.*

JULIE: We should have painted those walls together.

SOPHIA: That's all I've ever wanted.

JULIE: Kitten.

> SOPHIA *embraces* JULIE..

TONY: This is very confusing.

JULIE: Imagine me as—Chinese!

SOPHIA: Exactly!

GREG: Sophia, your mother is not Chinese!

SOPHIA: / But imagine if she was, that's all.

JULIE: You're an artist, Greg. Imagine me as Asian.

GREG: I'm not going to do that.

JULIE: But imagine if this family valued family—like a family.

GREG: I'm pretty sure this is a pretty racist analogy.

JULIE: Be silent, Greg! Don't cancel me! This country is so negatively geared! Sophia is right. We sold our soul for real estate!

TONY: Can we just chill for a second!

JULIE: And as for you, my husband!

TONY: Not the face.

JULIE: This … man. This *sales*man.

When I said 'I do' to your proposal, I thought we were investing in our future. Together. Fifty-fifty. But look at us! Vagabonds. Perched on the precipice of an old-age pension. Deep in the arse end of middle age and what have I got to show for all the blood and dinner-party stories of sacrifice?

TONY: Sweetheart, I've got you. You are everything I ever wanted.

My very own Big M Girl.

JULIE: Is that what you think I am?

*She takes the engagement ring off her own finger and holds it high.*

TONY: Hey, let's not get crazy!

JULIE: You think I'm crazy? This is not crazy!

*We hear thunder.*

TONY: That ring … !

JULIE *stands astride the crack. Angels and thunder and* TONY *screaming. In the anarchy we hear a ghostly 'America' by Simon and Garfunkel. Ensemble gather under* JULIE *like a biblical tableau, with* JULIE *holding the ring aloft in a storm. While the music and thunder crescendos we hear …*

JULIE: A noose! A contract! A deed of sale!

TONY: We married our fortunes together—

JULIE: I want a bloody refund!

*JULIE hurls the ring into the crack beneath her!*

*In almost slow-motion* SOPHIA *comes closer to* JULIE.

*GREG and* TONY *are prostrate on the floor near the crack.*

*We can hear 'America' more clearly, it's a gentle comedown.*

*JULIE begins to gently brush* SOPHIA's *hair.*

*They share silent secrets and laughter. When the music concludes.*

*JULIE finishes brushing* SOPHIA's *hair.*

Always so beautiful, Sophia.

TONY: [*quietly reflecting*] A lesson learned in stereo …

GREG: Can somebody turn the record over?

JULIE *kisses* SOPHIA.

SOPHIA: Thank you.

*Moment. Lights out.*

## THE END

RED STITCH

THE ACTORS' THEATRE

presents

# A Simple Act of Kindness

## 23 NOVEMBER–18 DECEMBER 2022

Playwright
**Ross Mueller**

Director
**Peter Houghton**

Set and Costume Design
**Jacob Battista and Sophie Woodward**

Lighting Design
**Amelia Lever Davidson**

Sound Design
**David Franzke**

Stage Manager
**Natasha Marich**

Assistant Stage Manager
**Douglas Hassack**

Assistant Lighting Design
**Sam Diamond**


Greg – **Khisraw Jones-Shukoor**

Tony – **Joe Petruzzi**

Julie – **Sarah Sutherland**

Sophia – **Lou Wall**


This play was developed through Red Stitch's INK writing program.

# RED STITCH

*We at Red Stitch acknowledge and pay our respects to Australia's First Peoples and Elders past and present, and offer our gratitude to the Boon Wurrung and Wurundjeri Woi Wurrung peoples of the Kulin Nation, on whose unceded lands we work.*

## THANK YOU

This development and production of *A Simple Act of Kindness* would not have been possible without the generous support of our donors and partners

## KINDRED DONORS

Andrew Domasevicius & Aida Tuciute
Jane & Stephen Hains & Portland House Foundation
The James Family Charitable Foundation
Maureen Wheeler AO & Tony Wheeler AO
Lyngala Foundation
Jane Hansen AO
Graham & Judy Hubbard
Graham Webster & Teri Snowdon
Beth Brown
Per & Ingrid Carlsen
Carrillo Gantner AC & ZiYin Gantner AC
Brian Goddard in Memoriam
John Haasz
The Neff Family
Rosemary Walls
Anonymous
Larry Abel
Caitlin English
Linda Herd
Liz & Peter Jones
Michael Kingston
Alex Lewenberg
The Lewis Langbroek Charitable Trust
The Mothers
Jenny Schwarz
The Kate & Stephen Shelmerdine Family Foundation
Christina Turner
Anonymous

# WRITER'S NOTE

This is the first play I've written for Red Stitch Actors Theatre.

It's also the first play I have written over Zoom. When we started the process, we were living in what we thought was a normal world. We were developing a kooky play about real estate and drilling into the notion that family is a series of transactions. Cynical, I know, right? But real estate is brutal and divisive. So the play was always going to be a hard arse comedy, and then the pandemic arrived.

I remember the day at Red Stitch when we were just about to do a reading or we'd just finished, I actually don't know for sure. But we were in the back room at Cromwell Road and the news began to break that the theatre industry was closing down. Going into hibernation.

We were suddenly on the precipice of an enormous cliff. We had no idea how long this would last and we had no idea of what would happen to normality.

If the play is about getting into the Market, then it is dealing with contemporary pressures. The pandemic was bringing a sledgehammer of reality. How much reality is too much reality? Will it overwhelm family? Will it steal the thunder of story? Will there be a happy ending or will we all be in lockdown forever?

We had a decision to make.

Another indistinct distinct memory is the Zoom call when Peter and Ella and I meet to make this decision. The light in the sky is a beautiful pink, the breeze is a whisper. We decided to move ahead and I think the play was scheduled to be performed at the end of 2021. (I think.)

Anyway, the development was conducted through lockdowns. A daisy chain of intercity Zooms. A pandemic way to work.

I want to thank Ella and Peter and the whole team of amazing actors at Red Stitch who committed to the realisation of this play. Every time we have been able to get into the same room at the same time, it has been a celebration of community. This is why I write for theatre. I love being in the same room with other people and laughing.

I love these characters with all my heart. I know them and I don't know them at all. I love they are not perfect, and I love they continually surprise me with brutality and a capacity to love and endure. Maybe that's the lesson I learned? My life is very different to when this whole thing started. Shaped and shifted by pressures and opportunities of prolonged isolation and escape.

I hope you enjoy this play. For me, everything has been worth it.

Thank you.

**Ross Mueller**
Playwright

# DIRECTOR'S NOTE

I first directed a play by Ross, *No Man's Island* back in 1997. It was a defining production for me and in many ways I owe a debt to the playwright for my own path since. Ross is a political writer, his view of the world and all the ways in which it could be better infuse his works in sometimes sly and sometimes overt ways. That early work was set in a prison and was embedded in a father-son relationship that touched many in the audience in a way that's rarely achieved. Eschewing the easy path of didactic preaching, he found a tone and two cyphers for our anxieties around masculinity that touched many in the audience with a gentle and encouraging hand. The play introduced a playwright with heart, intelligence, an excellent ear for dialogue and a highly developed social conscience. Twenty five years later he's written a pure comedy, with many doors, fulsome and hilarious characters, a heavily pregnant situation and all the other stuff that makes a comedy... a comedy!

Truth be told, I do love a comedy. I love the joy and the pain of making a joke work, of making a situation resonate precisely because of its excruciating familiarity or the total commitment of a character to an absurdity. This play has all that in spades. And of course being Ross, he also has something to say, which elevates the work from the fairy floss lightness of a true farce. The key to great comedy of course is not to skate on stereotype or find obvious fault with institutions but rather, to find fault with ourselves and to laugh at the ways in which we institutionalise our faults. In this play the target is our obsession with real estate, our confusion between the institution of the family home and our endless love of a hard asset. Ross salts this soup with a precarious tightrope walk over a void which reduces all interaction to some kind of algorithm-driven power play. Everything from our personal identities to our fashionable stances become chess pieces to be deployed in the complex game of defeating others and maintaining our own pompous but crumbling identities. Positioning seems more important than integrity and the home itself, that bastion of love and comfort is, in this competitive maelstrom, reduced to a receptacle for our vanities. So... what happens when the house of cards collapses, generations are reunited in cramped surroundings and futures are taken hostage by a global pandemic.

Hilarity hopefully.

Ross has delivered a provocative but hope-filled comedy. Our wonderful cast will find their inner fools and channel all our lovable but fatally flawed aspirations. This is a play that loves its characters, its audience and offers a telling parable for our not so brave new world. Most importantly it reaches out to all of us baffled and shell shocked individuals, not knowing where we want to be.

**Peter Houghton**
Director

# ROSS MUELLER
## PLAYWRIGHT

In 2002, Ross was the Australian playwright at the International Residency of the Royal Court Theatre in London. In 2007, *The Ghost Writer* premiered at Melbourne Theatre Company and *Construction of The Human Heart* was shortlisted for the AWGIE Award for Best New Play, the New York New Dramatists Award and was nominated for five Green Room Awards. Ross was the winner of the Wal Cherry Play of the year 2007 for his play, *The Glory*. His play, *Concussion*, won the 2008 New York Dramatists Award and premiered in 2009 at Sydney Theatre Company in co-production with Griffin Theatre. The same year, *Hard Core* was shortlisted for the Patrick White Award. *ZEBRA!*, featuring Bryan Brown, Nadine Garner and Colin Friels, premiered with a sell-out season at STC in 2011. In 2015, *A Town Named War Boy* was produced by ATYP at the State Library of NSW and he was commissioned by Malthouse Theatre to write *I Can't Even*, a monologue performed by Louise Siversen and Rhys Muldoon at the Malthouse Theatre. In 2017, *A Strategic Plan* premiered at Griffin Theatre and *Lifetime Guarantee* premiered at Theatre Works. The Street Theatre and the National War Memorial commissioned him to write *Epitaph* in 2018. Ross was commissioned by ABC Radio Fiction to write and co-direct a four-part romantic comedy series; *The Right Fit* in 2019 and again in 2020, to write and record monologues in response to the pandemic. He has written six plays for Radio National and had two books for children published with Allen and Unwin. He has been working with Vanessa Bates on the development of television series, *Troubled Youth*, supported by Screen Australia and Northern Pictures and *Love.Chaos.Theory* with Princess Pictures. He was the winner of the Georgi Markov Award as part of the BBC International Playwriting Prize in 2020.

# PETER HOUGHTON
## DIRECTOR

Peter has won numerous awards for his work including Green Room Awards for Best Actor for *The Pitch* and *Endgame*, Best Play for the *Pitch* and Best Director for his body of work. He has received awards from Melbourne and Edinburgh fringe festivals and his productions as director have received numerous awards and nominations. He was an MTC writer in residence and has lectured in performance and design at WAAPA, VCA and Monash. For Red Stitch: *The Way Things Work* (Actor). Theatre includes: As director: *Heartbreak Choir, The Architect, Boy at the Edge of Everything, True Minds, The Odd Couple, The Recruit, Hinterland, Art and Soul* (Melbourne Theatre Company); *The China Incident, Svetlana In Slingbacks, God's Last Acre* (Malthouse Theatre); *Day One a Hotel Evening* (Black Swan); *Footprints on Water* (Griffin Theatre); *Noises Off* (Marriner Theatres) *No Man's Island* (Melbourne Festival). As actor: *Macbeth, Misalliance, Birthrights, Laughter on the 23rd Floor, Sweet Bird of Youth, His Girl Friday, Joy Of Text, Shakespeare in Love, Three Little Words, Female of the Species, Hamlet Ex, Macbeth* (Melbourne Theatre Company); *The Trial* and *Travesties* (Sydney Theatre Company); *Tartuffe, The Pitch, Mr Melancholy, Tear From a Glass Eye, A View of Concrete, Ruby Moon* (Malthouse Theatre); *The Graduate* (Her Majesty's Theatre); *The Beast* (Ambassador Group); *North by Northwest* (Kay & McLean). As playwright: *The Pitch* (La Mama, Malthouse Theatre, Black Swan, Queensland Theatre, National tour UK); *The China Incident* and *A Commercial Farce* (Malthouse Theatre); *The Colours* (Melbourne Theatre Company). Film/television includes: As actor: *Utopia, Winners and Losers, Gallipoli, Hoges, Howzat, Killing Time, Newstopia, Neighbours, Wrong Kind of Black, Little Acorns, Wentworth, The Eye of the Storm, Little Oberon* and *Metal Skin,* among others.

## JACOB BATTISTA
### SET AND COSTUME DESIGN

Jacob Battista is a Melbourne-based theatre designer and practitioner. Jacob completed a Bachelor of Production at the Victorian College of the Arts. Some of his credits include, *Admissions* (MTC); *Grace, Iphigenia in Splott, Love, Love, Love, Jumpers for Goalposts, Belleville* and *Out Of The Water* (Red Stitch); *Hand to God, You're a Good Man Charlie Brown* and *Bad Jews* (Vass Theatre Group); *Rust and Bone* (La Mama Theatre); *Burn This* (fortyfivedownstairs); *Songs for a New World* (Blue Saint); *MEMBER* (Fairly Lucid); *Frankie and Johnny in the Clair De Lune* (Collette Mann/fortyfivedownstairs); *The Lonely Wolf* (Dirty Pretty Theatre/MTC Neon); *Therese Raquin* (Dirty Pretty Theatre); *Carrie The Musical* (Ghost Light); as associate set designer, *Shakespeare in Love* (Melbourne Theatre Company). Jacob (alongside Sophie Woodward) was nominated for two Green Room Awards in 2021 for *Iphigenia in Splott*. Jacob was a recipient of a 2016 Besen Family Scholarship at Malthouse Theatre working with Marg Horwell on *Edward II* and is also a recipient of an Australia Council ArtStart Grant.

## SOPHIE WOODWARD
### SET AND COSTUME DESIGN

Sophie is a Melbourne-based set and costume designer. Sophie graduated with a Bachelor of Production (Design) from VCA in 2010 winning the Beleura John Tallis Design Award in her final year. Sophie recently designed *Fast Food, Iphigenia in Splott* and *Grace* at Red Stitch Actors Theatre and was Costume Designer for *Come Rain or Come Shine* at MTC. Earlier design work from Sophie includes *Hungry Ghosts* (MTC); *Burn One, The One and Mr Burns, A Post Electric Play* (fortyfivedownstairs); *Those Who Fall in Love like Anchors Dropped Upon the Ocean Floor, Between* the Clouds, Pyjama Girl and Letters from the Border (Hothouse Theatre); Extinction, Rules for Living, You Got Older, Uncle Vanya, The Honey Bees, The Village Bike, Wet House, Love Love Love, 4,000 Miles and Day One, A Hotel, Evening (Red Stitch); Thigh Gap, A Long Day's Dying, Conspiracy, Patient 12 and The Savages of Wirramai (LaMama); Love Song (Melbourne Fringe); and The Sapphires, Glorious, Educating Rita, Shirley Valentine, Always Patsy Cline and All My Love (Hit Productions). Sophie was Design Assistant on An Ideal Husband and Twelfth Night (MTC). You can view Sophie's work at www.sophiewoodwarddesign.com

## AMELIA LEVER DAVIDSON
### LIGHTING DESIGN

Amelia Lever-Davidson is a multi award-winning lighting designer for theatre, dance, live art, installation and events. Amelia is a graduate of The Victorian College of the Arts, The Western Australian Academy of the Performing Arts and RMIT. Amelia has designed lighting for Sydney Theatre Company, The Melbourne Theatre Company, Belvoir St Theatre, Malthouse Theatre, Chunky Move, Red Stitch, Chamber Made, Elbow Room, Belarus Free Theatre, Deep Soulful Sweats, The Hayloft Project, MKA, Circa, and many others. She has collaborated with a diverse range of directors and choreographers including Susie Dee, Daniel Schlusser, Robin Fox, Yaron Lifschitz, Dean Bryant, Kate Champion, Declan Greene, Luke Kerridge, Janice Muller, Sarah Aiken, Martin Hansen, Prue Clark, Bridget Balodis, Gary Abrahams, Samara Hersch, Le Gateaux Chocolate, Adrienne Truscott, Lauren Langlois and Joel Bray. Amelia's work has been presented both nationally and internationally at festivals including Wuhzen Festival China, Perth, Melbourne, Brisbane and Darwin Festival, Dark MOFO, Dance Massive, Castlemaine Festival, Next Wave, FOLA, Melbourne, Perth, Adelaide Fringe Festival, Auckland Fringe, NZ Fringe Wellington and Edinburgh Fringe. Her design credits include *Julius Caesar* (STC); *Leviathan* (Circa); *Admissions, Torch the Place, The Violent Outburst that Drew me to You* (MTC); *My Brilliant Career, Every Brilliant Thing* (Belvoir); *Because the Night, Australian Realness, Trustees, Turbine* (Malthouse Theatre); *Myself in the Moment, System_Error, Diaspora* (Chamber Made); *Next Move* (Chunky Move); *Moral Panic, Contest, Niche, Conviction, Dream Home* (Darebin Speakeasy); *Hand to God* (Vass Productions); *Looking Glass, Triumph* (fortyfivedownstairs); *desert, 6:29pm; Jurassica; Foxfinder* (Red Stitch); *MKA's Double Feature* (MTC Neon); *Meta* (Malthouse Helium Season); *Ground Control, Camel, Hello There We've Been Waiting for You* (Next Wave Festival). As lighting associate: *The Nico Project* (Melbourne Festival). As tour lighting associate: *Minnie & Liraz* (MTC); *MKA's Double Feature* (MTC Neon); *Meta* (Malthouse Helium Season); *Ground Control, Camel, Hello There We've Been Waiting for You* (Next Wave Festival). Amelia's work has been recognised with Green Room Awards for *Diaspora, Contest, Looking Glass* and her 2015 body of work. Amelia is an Australia Council ArtStart and JUMP Mentorship recipient, Ian Potter Cultural Trust recipient, and a past participant in the Malthouse Besen Family Artist Program and the Melbourne Theatre Company's inaugural Women in Theatre Program. Amelia has also worked as a lighting director and lighting technician for Channel Ten, Channel Nine, the ABC, the National Gallery of Victoria and Fremantle Media. As lighting director, her work includes: *The Sunday Footy Show; TAC Future Stars; Kids WB; A Current Affair* and *National Nine News*. Amelia has undertaken mentorships with Paule Constable, Jon Clark, Paul Jackson, The Rabble, and international placements with Dewey Dell (Venice Biennale) and Hartley™ Kemp (Edinburgh Fringe Festival). Amelia is a founding member of The New Working Group, a network of independent artists, bringing together the creative output, ideas, resources and skills of writers, directors and designers to create a support structure for new work development and presentation.

## DAVID FRANZKE
### SOUND DESIGN

David Franzke is a composer and sound designer, music mixer and producer. His primary work is composing and designing for live performance in theatre. It also includes film, visual art installations as well as the production of albums. Known for his bold and idiosyncratic scores Franzke has worked with some of Australia's most influential directors including, Simon Phillips, Matthew Lutton, Peter Houghton, Marion Potts, Michael Kantor, Pamela Rabe and Richard Lowenstein. His work has toured both nationally and internationally. Franzke's work has been recognised with a 2021 Green Room Award for *Because The Night*, 2018 Green Room Award for composition and sound design for *Melancholia*, 2017 Green Room Award for Composition and Sound Design for *Away*, 2016 Green Room Award for *Picnic at Hanging Rock*, 2013 Green Room Award for *Pompeii L.A.* With a contribution spanning over 25 years in the arts industry of Australia, and his unique approach to each project, he continues to challenge and provoke audiences providing visceral experiences for audiences across many artforms.

## NATSASHA MARICH
### STAGE MANAGER

Natasha has enjoyed a long and varied career in the performing arts since the late '80s, working as a production assistant with the Melbourne Symphony Orchestra by day, and as a rock 'n' roll roadie by night. After graduating from NIDA, Natasha quickly established herself as a Touring Stage Manager with a strong focus on new works and has gained experience across a wide spectrum of disciplines: from puppetry, circus, contemporary dance, comedy, drama, and opera and has toured extensively around Australia and overseas. Professional highlights include productions with: the Prague Fringe Festival (2019), Keene/Taylor

Theatre Project, Handspan Theatre, Terrapin Puppet Theatre, Griffin Theatre, Playbox/Malthouse Theatre, writer/performer Eddie Perfect, writer/performer Angus Cerini, Pinchgut Opera, Chunky Move, Red Stitch Actors' Theatre, et al. In recent years, she realised her interests as an independent producer and in 2017-18 worked with Annette Shun Wah at Contemporary Asian Australian Performance (Sydney) and this year co-produced (with Hearth Theatre) the critically acclaimed production of *Death of a Salesman* at fortyfivedownstairs in Melbourne.

## DOUGLAS HASSACK
### ASSISTANT STAGE MANAGER

Douglas recently finished a Masters in creative arts at Deakin University during lockdown and was given the opportunity to perform his solo performance piece for the ADSA (Australasian Association for Theatre, Drama and Performance Studies) conference in 2021. He has been a volunteer stage manager for both *Masquerade Talent Studios* and *Masquerade Youth Productions* for a number of years, most recently with The first Australian performance of *Newsies JR*. In addition to this Douglas had the pleasure of assisting on *The Anniversary* by Salvador Dinosaur on the 2020 and 2022 seasons and soon to be seen in the La Mama Explorations Program in 2023. Theatre includes: *The Anniversary* (Salvador Dinosaur); *Fugitive Bodies: Marking the Horizon 2022* (Judith Walton); *Cinderella* (Masquerade Youth Production); *Newsies JR* (Masquerade Youth Production); *The Aristocats: Kids*; *Legally Blonde: JR*; *Into the Woods: Highschool*; *The Little Mermaid*; *Seussical: Kids*; *Dear Edwina: JR*; *The Addams Family: Highschool*; *Annie: Kids*; *Shrek: JR*; *Chicago: Highschool*; *A Chorus Line*; *Singing in the Rain: JR*; *The Lion King: Kids* (Masquerade Talent Studios).

## SAM DIAMOND
### ASSISTANT LIGHTING DESIGN

Sam is a Naarm/Melbourne-based set, costume and lighting designer. He is a graduate of the Master of Design for Performance from the Victorian College of the Arts where he was the recipient of the 2019 Orloff Family Charitable Trust Scholarship for excellence in production, and holds a Bachelor of Environmental Design (Architecture) from the University of Western Australia. Working at the intersection of form, space and light, Sam enjoys theatre most when it augments the fabric of space and time to create alternate realities and conceptual worlds through succinct, bold and transformative design. As the 2022 graduate designer with Red Stitch he is incredibly excited and proud to work with a company that continues to produce ambitious contemporary theatre, expanding the limits of what can be achieved on stage.

## KHISRAW JONES-SHUKOOR
### GREG

Khisraw's work includes *Because the Night* (Malthouse Theatre), *OIL* (Red Stitch), *Macbeth* (Melbourne Theatre Company), *FIERCE* (Theatre Works), *The Way Out* (Red Stitch), *THEM* at La Mama Courthouse (Green Room Award nominated for Best Ensemble), *Romeo and Juliet* (Australian Shakespeare Company) and *A Comedy of Errors* (Melbourne Shakespeare Company).

## JOE PETRUZZI
### TONY

Joe graduated from the National Institute of Dramatic Art (NIDA) in 1984 and from 1988–1990 furthered his training in New York at HB Studios. He has worked extensively in television and film both in Australia and overseas. Television credits include *The Devil's Playground* (TV Series) as well as ongoing roles in *Stingers, Possession*, and *The Violent Earth*. Joe has featured in *Bordertown* and *The Last Resort* (for the ABC), as well as appearances in *Rush, Neighbours, McLeod's Daughters, Salem's Lot, Blue Heelers, Beastmaster, Crash Palace, White Collar Blue, Water Rats, Police Rescue, On the Beach, All Saints, The Magistrate, Fields of Fire, Mafia Marriage*, and *Flipper*. Joe's film work includes *Love's Brother, Paws, The Real Macaw, Mambo Kings, Dingo, Citizen Cohn* and *Captain Johnno*. In 2017, Joe was invited to join the Red Stitch Actors' Ensemble after being involved in *Jurassica* (2015) and *The Village Bike* (2016). Since then, he has performed in *The Way Things Work* (2017), *American Song* (2017), *desert, 6:29pm* (2017), *Right Now* (2018) and *Fury* (2018). Most recently Joe was involved in *Prayer Machine* (2022), developed through the Red Stitch INK program for local writers.

## SARAH SUTHERLAND
### JULIE

Sarah joined the Red Stitch Actors Theatre ensemble in 2006 and has performed in many Red Stitch productions including: *Ulster American, Desert, 6:29pm, The Realistic Joneses, Day One. A Hotel. Evening, That Face, Faces In the Crowd, Red Sky Morning, After Miss Julie* and *Fewer Emergencies*. Other stage credits include leading roles in MTC's *Dead Man's Cell Phone* and *The Water Carriers*, and with The Flinders Quartet in *Behind Closed Doors*. On television Sarah is best known for her role as Kareena in *Angry Boys* for ABC/

BBC/HBO. Other credits include *Miss Fisher's Modern Murder Mysteries, Neighbours, Stingers, Blue Heelers* and numerous short films including *In Your Dreams, The Postman, The Director, When I Go, Carcass, The Cuckoo* and *The True History of Billy the Kid.* Sarah is the Artistic Director of Rollercoaster Theatre Company, a not for profit ensemble of neuro diverse and mixed ability actors. Over the 15 years she has been with Rollercoaster she has produced, directed and devised a great many productions including the multi-award-winning short film *Comican't.*

# LOU WALL
## SOPHIA

Lou Wall is a multi-award-winning comedian and writer based in Naarm. In 2020, Lou's film *Lousical the Musical* swept the Green Room Awards winning Best Production, Best Writing and Outstanding Online Achievement in Cabaret. The show also took out Melbourne Fringe's Best Cabaret Award. Over the past five years Lou's shows have been recognised for their genre bending, politically savvy comedy and garnered critical acclaim. Their works include black comedy cabaret *A Dingo Ate My Baby* (Malthouse Theatre, MICF); *It's Not Me, It's Lou* (Melbourne Cabaret Festival's Emerging Cabaret Artist Award; Best Cabaret Award nominee, Melbourne Fringe); *Romeo Is Not The Only Fruit* (Green Room Award nominee; Brisbane Festival, Malthouse Theatre MICF) and *Lou Wall's Drag Race* (Griffin Theatre, Best Emerging Artist Melbourne Fringe). For TV, Lou has featured in ABC America's *Reef Break* and ABC Australia's *FISK* alongside Kitty Flannagan. In 2021, Lou's solo show *That One Time I Joined The Illuminati* was nominated for three Green Room Awards and took out two artist development awards at Melbourne Fringe. In 2022, Lou wrote a comedy album called *Bleep Bloop* and is currently penning an original musical with their long time collaborators (Jean Tong and James Gales) called *Flat-Earthers: The Musical.*

## RED STITCH ACTORS' THEATRE

We are an actor-led ensemble, enriching our community by empowering artists as cultural leaders. We inspire audiences with compelling contemporary theatre that engages with the complexities of humanity and reveals us to ourselves. Our organisational model nurtures artistic vibrancy and growth.

Red Stitch is a creative hub, offering scope for artists to make work they are passionate about in a sector where such opportunities are limited. As the ensemble and executives of Red Stitch, we provide a platform where leading practitioners can hone their craft and take risks, and emerging artists can work alongside mid-career and seasoned professionals. We play a vital role in the development and presentation of new Australian works through our INK playwriting program, promoting local voices alongside acclaimed contemporary international work which may not otherwise be seen by local audiences.

**www.redstitch.net**

Red Stitch would like to thank the following supporters who generously contribute to our INK program.

**Australian Government**
**RISE Fund**

**CREATIVE VICTORIA**

CITY OF PORT PHILLIP

Cybec Foundation

MALCOLM ROBERTSON FOUNDATION

THE PORTLAND HOUSE FOUNDATION

PLAYKING FOUNDATION

Lyngala Foundation

THE MYER FOUNDATION

SIDNEY MYER FUND

Kindred